# Coaching
# Mental
# Excellence

**Ralph Vernacchia** is a Professor of Physical Education in the Department of Physical Education, Health, and Recreation at Western Washington University where he directs the undergraduate and graduate programs in sport and exercise psychology. He has presented research on a variety of sport psychology topics throughout the nation and is a certified consultant (AAASP). He serves as a performance consultant to the Western Washington University Athletic Department and is a co-chair for the Sport Psychology Sub-Committee of USA Track and Field. He has traveled internationally as a performance consultant with several U. S. track and field teams and serves as sport psychology curriculum chair and an instructor for the USA Track and Field National Coaching Education program. He was a track and field coach for twenty-two years.

**Rick McGuire** is the Head Track and Field Coach at the University of Missouri, where he has led his teams and athletes to positions of prominence, producing Olympic medalists, national champions, collegiate record holders, and literally dozens of All-American athletes. Of even greater significance, his athletes are champions in the classroom as well, earning numerous academic All-American designations, Phi Beta Kappa awards, and post-graduate fellowships. Dr. McGuire also serves as a member of the graduate faculty in the university's College of Education. He is the chairman of sport psychology for USA Track and Field, and has served as sport psychologist for many U. S. national track and field teams in major international competitions. He also works with Basketball Canada's national men's and women's teams, and with PGA touring professionals.

**David Cook** is the Director of Applied Sport Psychology at the University of Kansas where he serves as sport psychologist for eighteen varsity sports and directs the graduate program in sport psychology. Dr. Cook has established himself as one of the nation's leading applied sport psychologists. He recently served as president of the National Sport Psychology Academy. His clients have included athletes from the 1988 NCAA basketball championship team, the 1987 World Series championship team, the National Football League, Major League Baseball, the National Basketball Association, the World Championship Track and Field meet, and the PGA, Senior PGA, and LPGA tours. Dr. Cook also serves as the U. S. Olympic pole vault group sport psychologist.

# Coaching
# Mental
# Excellence

## It DOES matter whether you win or lose

**Ralph A. Vernacchia, Ph.D.**
Western Washington University

**Rick T. McGuire, Ph.D.**
University of Missouri

**David L. Cook, Ph.D.**
University of Kansas

Warde Publishers, Inc.

Portola Valley, California

Warde Publishers, Inc.
3000 Alpine Road
Portola Valley, CA 94028
(800) 699–2733

*Library of Congress Cataloging-in-Publication Data*
Vernacchia, Ralph A., 1945–
      Coaching mental excellence : it does matter whether you win or lose . . . / Ralph Vernacchia, Rick McGuire, David Cook.
            p.      cm.
      Includes index.

*Library of Congress Catalog Card Number:* 95-61796
ISBN 1-886346-02-X

Printed in the United States of America

10   9   8   7   6   5   4   3   2      98   97

Design: Detta Penna

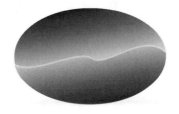

# Dedication

*To the memory of my mother, Anne Vernacchia, and to my father, Ralph Vernacchia, with love, respect, appreciation, and admiration.*

RAV

*To the memory of the late Coach Robert Kana*
  *. . . teacher, coach, and athletic director;*
  *. . . who brought the joy and excitement of sport to generations of youngsters;*
  *. . . whose leadership was an inspiration for thousands;*
  *. . . and, whose footsteps I have humbly attempted to follow.*
*May this work, and all that I do through sport, add greater luster to the legacy he has left.*

RM

*I would like to acknowledge the coaches who helped me shape my life and who ignited the competitive fire that has yet to dim. Thanks Reggie Davis, Maurice Varnell, and Jack Gibson. You'll never know the profound impact that you have had on my life. I would also like to acknowledge the best coach I ever had, the man who had the greatest impact on my life, my dad, Charles Cook. To each of you, thanks, your influence was appreciated.*

DC

# Contents

# Preface

In the summer of 1986, a unique five-day meeting took place at the United States Olympic Training Center in Colorado Springs. Several of the nation's most respected coaches met with several of the nation's top sport psychologists to discuss and develop an applied sport psychology curriculum for a national coaching education program.

The task at hand was to develop an outline of the most important topics within sport psychology according to the needs of the coaching profession. As the coaches shared their heartfelt concerns about their profession, it became clear that their needs went beyond the typical coach-athlete issues, to the issues of coach and family, coach and staff, and coach and self. Many of the topics which were raised have been given minimal attention in the "Psychology of Coaching" literature. It became very obvious that coaches had needs from the sport psychology profession which weren't currently being addressed in a practical manner.

The three authors of this book chaired the meeting and were charged with developing educational materials in the form of a national coaching education curriculum, coaching workshops, workshop outlines, and eventually a book on the topics which were generated from the five days of discussion at the USOTC.

Thus, several years of research, teaching, writing and interactions with coaches have resulted in the publication of this book. It is our sincere desire that the lives of coaches will be enhanced and enriched through the material contained within these pages. Coaching is a unique profession which allows unlimited influence on the lives of our nation's most important resources, our youth. We need to recruit, develop, and retain great coaches who lead by positive example, while at the same time avoiding professional and personal burnout, and broken relationships at home and within their staffs. We need coaches who have the ability to keep sport in perspective so that their families receive the best they have to offer when they walk through the front door after fulfilling their on-the-field responsibilities as sport educators.

# Part I

# The Role and Influence of the Coach

# The Coach, Someone Special

The world of athletics is an exciting, energy-packed source of involvement, enjoyment, and entertainment for many. For players, parents, officials, administrators, boosters, and spectators, sport offers a meaningful focus for an important part of their lives, and an outlet from the drudgery, frustration, and pressures of daily activities.

At the very hub of all athletic activity are the coaches—men and women who form the nucleus, giving life to the sport experience. They play the single most important role in shaping the successes or failures, satisfactions or frustrations, and joys or sadness of the sport experience for the youngsters who run, jump, swim, shoot, kick, hit, throw or catch.

## The Coach

Becoming a coach marks the fulfillment of a valued goal and dream for many people. And yet, to be a coach, that is, to be all that is required of those in the position, is to possess many skills and abilities, to own great knowledge and wisdom, to be perceptive and understanding, and to be driven by an emotional commitment to sport, to self, and to others. Although this commitment may arise from a sometimes seemingly bottomless well of internal energy, to become a coach does not mean that one must be "super-human." But make no mistake, coaching is not for everyone. It is not just a position to which one is named or a title which one claims, but rather a stature and an honor which is earned. For to be "the Coach" is to be someone very special!

There is no one mold into which a coach must fit. Coaches may be young or old, short or tall, plump or thin, male or female, ex-athlete or non-athlete. They may be full-time or part-time, paid or unpaid, well-educated or not, rich or poor. But while coaches may be a diverse group, they share a pride and enthusiasm for sport, for their role as a coach, and, above all else, for their athletes.

Sport is played at many different levels, from Biddy-Ball and church league to Little Leagues and high schools, even on to the collegiate and professional ranks. Competitions may be within a school or community, or may be at a league, district, regional, state, national, or even international level. There may be wide ranges in age, size, interests, and abilities of the athletes, and in the quantity and quality of available equipment and facilities. But, wherever and however it is played, sport and the role of the coach remain fundamentally the same.

For those who have coached, special chords of emotion are struck when they remember the first practice of the new season, the noise and atmosphere unique to the long rides on the team bus, the "smells" of the locker room, the opening of the gym in the early morning hours, or closing it very late at night, budget cuts and rain-outs, lining the field, the over-time victory (or loss), that first championship trophy, or the many talks at the annual athletic banquets.

But more than anything, the coach's thoughts are filled with memories of the kids, the athletes, the "people" of sport and long talks after practice, the sharing of dreams, both for sport and life; the reality of serious injury and the support and encouragement to come back... the sharing of success, the goal accomplished and the victory attained, or the comforting and drawing together after meeting defeat or failure... the counseling in time of personal strife or conflict, of having "been there" when needed most. It is this aspect of sport, the close , intimate relationships that are formed with others, that makes being a coach so rewarding and personally gratifying.

While skeptics may say that this idealistic or romantic view of coaching "is nice, but it doesn't win ballgames," the experiences of great and successful coaches have consistently shown that this attention to the athlete, the person, is the key to unlocking the door to athletic abilities and potentials. By producing athletes and teams who, individually and together, play consistently as well as they can, coaches also insure the greatest likelihood of gaining victories.

Coaches of today's and tomorrow's athletes will need this understanding of and commitment to the individuals with whom they work, as well as the knowledge of sound scientific principles relative to sport and coaching. The ideas presented in this chapter and throughout this text will provide such a scientifically based and experientially sound approach to the psychology of coaching. Topics and concepts presented in this book are consistently organized around an athlete-oriented philosophy founded in developmental psychology.

It is our intent as authors, to provide a psychological approach to coaching based on the creation of an environment filled with caring, trust, communication, and commitment between coaches and athletes. We believe that such an orientation will provide the very best that sport has to offer to both the athletes and coach.

## Sport—What Is It?

While some scholars and texts go to great lengths to clearly define and differentiate among concepts of play, games, sport, and athletics, such will not be the case here. Sport will be viewed in the rather classical context of individuals or groups, participating in physical activity involving the performance of a specific skill. Sport is generally characterized by some form of competition, either with self or others, and it is the uncertainty of the outcome of this competition that provides so much of the challenge and interest inherent in sport participation.

As was pointed out previously, sport is played at many levels by individuals with abilities ranging from novice to expert. While the roles and approaches of coaches may necessarily vary to some degree to meet appropriate needs of these various levels of sport, the fundamental concepts of successful coaching remain unchanged throughout sport.

Rather than attempting to define sport further, our purpose would be better served by examining the various roles sport plays in the lives of its participants and analyzing the roles that the coach must fulfill for sport to be a successful experience for all.

# The Role of Sport in the Life of the Athlete

Sport provides a variety of opportunities and plays several roles in the lives of athletes. All athletes are unique individuals and, as such, they are different in their approach to sport participation, in their desires, interests, involvements, and commitments. At the same time, sport provides many of the same things to all athletes, regardless of age, size, position, or ability.

By recognizing and understanding the many roles that sport plays for its athletes, coaches may best provide an exciting, enriching, and enjoyable sport experience.

## Sport is a Physical Activity

At the most obvious level, sport provides an opportunity for physical activity. This can involve the development of strength and physical fitness, the learning of new and more sophisticated motor skills, the release of energy and the chance to experience the simple enjoyment of movement. To run, jump, throw, and hit; to push and pull, pitch, and catch; to sweat and strain; and to relax—these are all a part of sport. Athletes come to better understand their bodies, the process of conditioning, the benefits of proper nutrition, and the lifelong implications of physical activity for enhancing health and happiness. At the bottom line, sport is physical!

## Sport is a Social Activity

Sport provides a social environment, an opportunity to meet new people and establish friendships. In the sport setting, athletes may learn to work successfully with others, to gain respect for differences in philosophies, values, temperaments, and convictions. Participants are exposed to authority figures and to the chain of command concept, and must learn to balance individual and group goals and aspirations.

Sport allows athletes the chance to share with others the struggle for success, the satisfaction and joy of having succeeded, and, of course, the pain, disappointment, and sorrow when their individual and collective efforts come up short of the aspired mark.

The sport setting provides an excellent opportunity for athletes to learn about and to deal with others.

## Sport and Identity

And while sport allows athletes to learn about others, it also provides them with experiences from which they can come to better understand themselves, to establish their own identity. Sport and sport participation are highly valued in our society, and to be identified as an athlete, or as being athletic, is a prized and coveted aspiration of many persons. To test one's self against both self and others, to experience success and failure, to taste both joy and despair, to feel satisfaction and frustration, to step into the unknown and to stretch one's self beyond presumed limits, to rethink one's values, to experience disillusionment and to have it replaced with re-affirmation, to move from doubt and fear to confidence and courage—these are all ingredients in one's search for self. And, they are all a very real part of sport.

## Sport, Dreams, and Fantasies

It is often said that dreams and fantasies are the world of children. What is left unsaid is that often these children are 25, 45, or even 85 years old. Certainly, millions of athletes, young and old, have practiced alone in the backyard, in the driveway, or even in the living room, and dreamed of making the winning shot in the championship game, catching the last-second pass for the winning touchdown, surging to the finish line to capture the gold medal, making the curling 50-foot putt for birdie, serving the ace at set point, or hitting the grand-slam home run in the bottom of the ninth. As these thoughts have played vividly in their minds, these athletes are captured by the magic of sport, the exhilaration of how great sport really could be, if only . . . !

## The Reality of Sport

Though sport fuels the athlete's flight into fantasy, it also presents a meaningful laboratory experience for recognizing and dealing with reality. To gain a measure of one's talents, to discover strengths and identify weaknesses, to learn to utilize one's capabilities while minimizing the negative effects of personal limitations, to develop an understanding of the process of persistence, while recognizing that hard work and dedication do not always assure success, to meet defeat and frustration as well as victory and satisfaction, to experience the joys of social favor and adulation, or the isolation and despair of disinterest and rejection—these all are significant products of the world of athletics.

While sport can appear to be an unreal world of fantasies, few athletes escape the valuable encounter with reality. Those who are not talented enough, strong enough, or determined enough, seldom succeed and "make it." And at one time or another, whether through freak injury, unfortunate draw, or devious politics, everyone learns that sport, like life, is not always fair!

## The Importance of Sport to the Athlete

Because of the pervasive influence of sport in the lives of athletes, sport is valued as holding great importance by many participants. Sport is fun and provides enjoyment and and an opportunity for good times with others. It offers a testing ground where athletes gain a sense of competence, achievement, and recognition.

Sport allows athletes to establish, test, and better understand their own values, and generally plays a vital role in the individual's personal growth and development. For many, sport can, at times, be the dominant experience and activity of life, perhaps exerting a greater influence even than family. It is the recognition of this level of significance in the lives of young athletes, then, that makes the role of those providing the leadership for sport so incredibly vital. The burden of this leadership responsibility rests squarely on the shoulders of the coach.

## The Role of the Coach in Sport

The role of the coach is, in fact, not a role at all, but rather many, many roles. The coach wears many different hats, which sometimes causes conflict and strain.

From the standpoint of the *program*, the coach must be an administrator, personnel manager, public relations and sales person, diplomat, strategist and tactician, recruiter and trainer, psychologist, judge, and above all else, a caring and committed teacher.

For the *athlete*, the coach is a leader, role model, and disciplinarian. The coach may be seen as a friend, counselor, or parent substitute, perhaps as close as a member of the family. The coach is the wizard who holds the key that unlocks the magic of the athletic dreams.

*Parents* of athletes expect the coach to play many of the same previously mentioned roles, and generally desire that the coach be committed to their children and to providing them with a fair opportunity to develop and display their athletic skills.

Quite naturally, parents desire to see their child excel, to get more playing time, or to be the star performer! But by and large, parents hope for sport to be a positive experience for their children. To this end, they expect the coach to provide caring, committed leadership and counsel, to be an enthusiastic role model who is proud of and excited about their children, and to offer an athletic experience which provides a fair opportunity for youngsters to develop physically, psychologically, and emotionally.

In all of these roles, coaches must be aware of their very special role as a "giver" or "provider." For a reality of sport is that the quality of the sport experience for all athletes, whether "Super-star, Steady Stevie, or Slew Foot," will likely be no better than the personal, moral, and leadership qualities of the coach who is providing that experience.

Certainly, the physical capabilities and motivations of the athletes are also key factors, as are the relative abilities of teammates and rivals, the quality of available equipment, facilities, and competitive opportunities, and even luck. But, far and away the single greatest determining factor of the quality of the athlete's sport experience is the coach. It is at the coach that athlete and athletics meet, and it is the coach who makes or breaks the child's athletic adventure.

Given the priority society in general and parents in particular place on our youth, and given the similar priority placed upon sport participation and achievement, the tremendous responsibility and challenge which accrues to anyone wishing to carry the title, "Coach," becomes readily apparent.

How does one meet this challenge? How do we best fulfill the demands of this nearly sacred responsibility? What is it that athletes, parents, and the sport world need from the coach?

## What the World of Sport Needs from the Coach

Great coaches, and by that we mean not just "famous" coaches, but rather coaches who have imparted a profound, positive influence on their teams and athletes, are consistently characterized by great levels of trust and respect in their relationships with others. These spring, not by accident or as a result of on the field successes, but rather from the very identifiable qualities and nature of the coach as a person. Idealism, enthusiasm, excitement, desire, determination, dedication, care, concern, compassion, and a genuine love for sport, and the athlete's career—these are all characteristic of most highly successful coaches.

Three keys to the athletic success of most great coaches are anticipation, preparation, and dedication to the pursuit of excellence. When preparing themselves, their teams, or their individual athletes for upcoming seasons or contests, superior coaches consistently are thorough in their anticipation of every possible situation which they might face. They then become engrossed in devising appropriate strategies to meet the challenges, and dedicated to achieving success in their athletic pursuits. In sport, this is commonly referred to as "Paying the Price." For the coach, this price includes the willingness to give freely, with great commitment of one's time, energy, and emotion.

Coaching is one of the greatest careers to which one can aspire. Our children need good coaches. Rather, they deserve to have great coaches, coaches who are filled with enthusiasm, energy, and love. They deserve coaches who are dedicated to providing the best possible experience through sport and who are committed to training happy, successful athletes, but more importantly, to inspiring and developing proud, motivated, successful, and happy young people. In short, we need coaches who are willing to "Pay the Price" themselves!!

# What Is There For The Coach?

What can the coach legitimately expect in return for this great personal investment? Are fame and fortune the reward for hard work and dedicated service? Very often they are not.

While a small few parlay sideline success into great financial wealth and garner public acclaim, only the naive or grossly misinformed enter coaching for these tangible but elusive benefits. Most coaches experience the reality of being underpaid, and often even unpaid, for their very valuable and valued services. And yet, hundreds and thousands of men and women willingly, enthusiastically and proudly join the coaching ranks each year. Why?

For many, often former or erstwhile athletes, it is the opportunity to remain close to the game, to continue in the competitive environment, to maintain the close associations and camaraderie, both with the athletes and fellow coaches, that abounds in the sport setting. Coaching offers challenges and opportunities to prove one's talents and abilities, to "find a better way," and to out-prepare, out-play or out-wit one's opponents.

Coaching may even give rise to business or professional contacts, and is often an entree into positions of community leadership. And, although few coaches receive national recognition or acclaim, many attain very enviable positions of local or regional prominence, and are accorded much respect and appreciation.

But above all else, most great coaches concur that the greatest reward they ever receive from coaching is the satisfaction of having played a very real part in the physical and personal development of the young people with whom they have worked. To have shared in these athletes' lives, their hopes and dreams, their joys and frustrations, their successes and failures, to have struggled, sweated, and suffered, to have educated, encouraged, and enjoyed, these are the spindles on which the coach-athlete relationship is spun. And, it is from these experiences that the coach draws the greatest reward and satisfaction. The money will be spent, the trophies do, in fact, become "tarnished and worn," and the newspaper clippings will turn yellow and wrinkle, but the investment in and commitment to the athletes yield benefits and dividends that multiply and grow in the lives of coaches and athletes.

The rewards of coaching, then, are measured not in what one is able to "get," but rather in the opportunities the coach has to "give" to others, to the athletes, to the kids. Whether seen in the smile on a youngster's face, a special glance or a twinkle of the eye, the answer to the question "Why coaches coach?" is found there, in the lives and growth of the athletes. And for those athletes, that coach is always someone very special. To meet years later, and to be greeted with a "Hi, Coach!"... there's nothing like it!!!

## The Challenge—Dare To Be Better

Yes, being a coach really can be great! In fact, coaching may be one of the most rewarding and gratifying professions. To provide for the growth and development of youngsters through their sport involvement, to give and receive trust and respect, and to influence others in their quest to become happy, healthy, and fulfilled individuals is an honor. It is also an immense challenge and responsibility. To meet this challenge, coaches must have the required knowledge and understanding, but more importantly, they must be armed with the desire to "Dare to be Better!!!"

Coaches must not only be able to recognize what individuals, teams, and the sport setting need and demand, but also confidently believe that their contributions will be better, and produce more positive benefits, than if that same experience were provided by someone else. Although not necessarily stated openly, this belief represents the pride and self-confidence which are necessary qualities for great leaders, and in sport, for great coaches.

The remaining chapters are devoted to identifying the critical psychological issues involved in coaching and athletics, to analyzing the relevant variables affecting or influencing each issue, to considering the coach's role in each or these issues, and to establishing appropriate and effective strategies for generating success and satisfaction from sport for everyone—the athletes, teams, families, community, and the coach!

Notice the inclusion of the last phrase, "… and the coach!" While coaching can be tremendously rewarding and satisfying, to be a great coach may also be extremely demanding, challenging, and physically, mentally and emotionally exhausting. It is not only the intent of this book to aid the coach in helping others achieve great success and pleasure through sport but to also insure that these same measures of satisfaction and enjoyment are realities in the coach's life as well.

We encourage you, then, to read on, to open your mind and heart to new questions, concepts, and ideas, and to grow in your desire and belief that you can become a great, great coach, that you, too, "Dare to be Better!" Know the excitement and exhilaration of continuing your life in sport, know the impact of the influence on those with whom you work, and know that to be "the Coach" is truly to be someone very special!

# The Coach's Philosophy

## Establishing Foundational Beliefs: "It Does Matter Whether You Win or Lose ..."

Any great religion, any established philosophy or enduring system of thought is characterized by a few key principles, short but powerful statements, that embody the essential truths of that religious or philosophical system. These are the foundational beliefs upon which everything else within the system is built. Without such foundational beliefs, a consistent, strong, and enduring structure cannot be built. The same holds true for sport and for coaches.

## Athletes Meet Sport at the Coach

The coach is the definer, creator, provider, and delivers the sport experience to the athlete. The sport experience is necessarily a direct reflection of the coach, and of the coach's philosophy, beliefs, values, principles, and priorities. The quality of an athlete's experience can never exceed the quality of the leadership providing it.

The romantic view of sport and sport participation suggests that sport can provide an experience of high ideals and valued virtues, that it may be one of the most positive influences in a youngster's life. Experience and observation, however, show clearly that such is not always the case. For example, for every athlete who has learned pride, many others have found shame. Ideally, athletes learn to respect others, but many participants become disrespectful, angry, and revengeful. And, while some might contend that sport teaches confidence and courage, too many athletes experience doubt and fear as sport participants.

Sport, by itself, doesn't guarantee that these, or any of the many other values generally ascribed to the sport experience, will in fact live in the reality of its participants. This depends primarily on the coach!

For coaches to play a constructive role in the lives of athletes, they must know what they value, and understand that these values will determine the quality of the sport experience. In short, it is critical for all coaches to possess their own personal philosophy of sport and coaching, characterized by a few specific "foundational beliefs." These fundamental principles provide the framework that, more than anything, determine how the coach provides, and what the athlete receives from the sport experience.

This chapter focuses on the development of coaches' foundational beliefs. While challenging coaches to identify their own foundational beliefs, those upon which this text are based are also provided.

*"It does matter whether you win or lose ...!"*

# Winning vs. Success

So much of what we see, hear about, and experience in sport is focused upon an athlete or a team of athletes attempting to gain a victory over others. Whether measured in running faster, jumping higher, scoring more points, using fewer strokes, or being more accurate, for many the focal issue in the competitive sport setting is winning.

Society tells youngsters, and even adults, that to be an athlete, is good. To be a winning athlete is even better. And to win a lot, even to become the champion, is great! Clearly, both directly and implicitly, sport participants are taught that winning is important.

To the winner, to gain the victory, many variables must come together in just the right combination. To list and analyze all of these variables would be very lengthy and difficult. However, such a factor analysis would reveal that there exist two primary factors that determine whether or not an individual or team will win. Two factors, more than any others lead to winning:

1. *How well we do at gaining from ourselves ALL that we are capable of delivering!*

Obviously, each individual athlete or team has a certain level of capability. How well one taps that capability and delivers all that is possible will go a long way toward determining whether or not a win is achieved. In short, how well one plays is the chief factor in winning. Anything short of one's best leaves the door open for defeat.

2. *Scheduling!*

As trite as it may seem, the second most important factor in winning is being scheduled to compete against someone of less capability. This is not to discount the time honored cliché of sport, that "... on any given day...." True, in spite of careful scheduling inferior teams and athletes can upset far superior teams. Still, the reality of the powerful role of scheduling in influencing a season's winning or losing record is inarguable.

With little question, these two factors clearly contribute enormously to the determination of who is the winner. Once the schedule is determined, however, the absolute determining factor is, "The ability to be consistently at our best in each competitive situation." If we play the best we possibly can, and if we schedule someone we are capable of beating, we probably will win. Probably, but not surely.

At best, winning is elusive. In fact, it is the uncertainty of the outcome, the mystery and anticipation of creating the desired outcome, that gives sport much of its spice, flavor, and intrigue. To win becomes the challenge.

But realistically, in any competitive sport setting, at best only 50 percent of the participants can be winners. In many competitions such as golf or tennis tournaments, cross country races, and diving competitions, only one participant gains the victory. Are all the participants losers? Is there no opportunity for fun, fulfillment, satisfaction, pride, and achievement without winning?

Is winning really the ultimate goal of sport, or is there possibly a higher value, a more important motive, and a goal that is attainable by all? If winning is measured in scoring more points or running faster, what then determines success? Can one not win, and still be a success? The answer, most assuredly is YES!

## What Is Success?

While only a very few may win in any competitive environment, success is available to everyone. Success is not determined by how well one does against another, but rather is measured only against oneself. Success can be understood as a product of four essential factors:

| **SUCCESS = Ability × Preparation × Effort × Will** |
| --- |

### Ability

Everyone has ability. Some have great cognitive abilities, while others have significant musical or artistic abilities. Others may have great motor or athletic abilities. While we each may have varying degrees of ability in certain areas, few if any have great abilities in all areas. We must also realize that ability is inherited.

Ability, sometimes called talent, is a gift which is acquired through our parents. While this is a reality, it is often a difficult and humbling realization for many. Finally, while having a lot of ability certainly enhances a person's opportunities to achieve in specific areas or activities, ability alone does not guarantee the attainment of success. Just being talented isn't enough, but rather how one develops and uses his or her talents will determine the level of success which is achieved. Thus, the need for preparation is clear.

## Preparation

Having talent and ability is one thing. Being able to utilize one's ability most effectively and efficiently is something altogether different. This occurs only after the committed investment of oneself in planned and purposeful preparation. This preparation, in sport called 'practice', leads to the development of natural abilities into greater levels of capability. Such developed capabilities may be reflected in greater speed, increased strength or more coordinated skills and movements. It also may include acquired knowledge and more insightful understanding. This developed capability allows for the access and use of more of one's natural ability, tapping more of that nebulous concept known as 'potential', and increasing an individual's opportunity to achieve.

But again, just having enough ability and having worked long and hard to develop greater capability doesn't insure either winning or success. Now this capability must be delivered in the competitive arena. It must be utilized. The game must now be played. How is our capability delivered? Through giving great effort!

## Effort

Now we're getting somewhere. Taking whatever abilities we have, and working hard in preparation to become more skilled and more capable than we have ever been before are truly important and necessary ingredients in becoming a success. But to put this capability to its best use in competitive athletics requires that individuals give great effort, to literally give as much of themselves as they possibly can. In sport, this is often referred to as "hustle." Certainly, the greatest effort and the use of one's capabilities will best insure a victory or success. Lack of great effort will surely result in diminished performance, and increase the possibility for defeat.

But even taking our ability, working hard in preparation, and giving great effort in the competitive arena won't always insure success. There is still one factor missing from the success equation—one's own will.

## Will

Anyone who has ever been a serious participant in sport has experienced the equivalent of the final two minutes of the football game. You have the ball on your own 20-yard line, no timeouts left, and your team is down by two points. Or, you are coming off the final turn in the mile race at the conference championships, you feel like you've spent every ounce of energy available, and then, with just 80 yards to go, an opponent pulls up on your shoulder and offers a strong challenge. Each of these situations represents "crunch time," the ultimate test and challenge of sport. There are times when you think that you've given all that you have only to find that even more is required. It is at this point that many a contest is won or lost. It is at this point that some competitors are able to draw upon an inner strength and to summon up an even greater effort, an effort which they may never have believed themselves capable of exerting.

This is the use of one's will. It involves one's will power, the willingness to choose to go back to that personal reservoir again, and again, and even again one more time if necessary. When individuals have done all of this, when they have taken whatever abilities they were given, worked persistently to prepare themselves to be as capable as they could possibly be at that point in time, went into the competitive arena and gave the greatest effort they could possibly deliver, and then, when they met "crunch time," when it was on the line, they chose to dig down even deeper and find the way to give even a little more, then regardless of outcome, they *are* a SUCCESS! What more could they do?

Let's make a more personal application. It is your child, your own son or daughter who is approaching the starting line for the final of the 800-meter race in the State High School Track Championships. You know what kind of talent your child has because he or she received that talent from you! You also know how hard he or she has worked to prepare for this day and this race. You've watched your child arise early every day to log miles on morning runs, and you've picked him or her up late after school after completing those daily training sessions on the track. You've watched your child overcome sore muscles, blisters, and sickness. You know that your child has given up many of the social activities that his or her friends have enjoyed to become thoroughly prepared for this challenge, this race. And you know that your child is going to the line . . . ready!

The leaders go through the first lap at a quick pace, and your son or daughter is right at the front, running strongly and comfortably. As they round the turn and head up the backstretch, your child breaks from the lead pack and begins to pick up the pace and lengthen the lead. Your child is giving the greatest effort of his or her life.

As your child approaches the last curve, he or she visibly begins to tire and tighten-up. The pack of runners behind your child begins to close the gap, and it appears that they will overtake your child. As the second place runner pulls even with your child's shoulder and makes a strong move to pass, your child responds and digs deep. He or she holds off the challenge and comes off the turn into the homestretch still in the lead. As the runners race for the finish line, the competitor on the outside sprints to the front and challenges your child for the lead. Again, he or she finds another gear, another reserve of energy that neither your child nor you thought could possibly be there, and once again holds off the challenge and maintains the lead.

With less than 20 meters to go, just as it appears that your child has the race won, yet another runner makes a desperate dash to take both the lead and the victory. In fact, this challenger appears to establish a slight lead over your child. Both athletes are fighting fatigue and straining to exact every last ounce of effort from their spent bodies, and as they breast the finish line, your child. . .

Do you need to know? Is it important? Do you need to know who won this race, to know whether or not you are a proud parent? Do you need to see the photo of the finish to determine if you are filled with love and joy for this youngster? Do you need to know who got to the line first before you can know whether or not your son or daughter is a success? Does he or she need to have the win before you will be able to offer congratulations and hugs for a job well done? Should your child's coach know that he or she just did a great job and ran a great race and that we're all proud of him or her, or are these accolades reserved only for the winner?

What more could this young athlete have done? The answer of course is. . . nothing! And for that, he or she is a total SUCCESS!

$$SUCCESS = Ability \times Preparation \times Effort \times Will$$

Success comes from taking whatever capabilities we possess and using them most effectively. There are identifiable characteristics which are directly related to being an effective individual, thus supporting and relating to becoming successful coaches and athletes.

Winning is available only to a few and only once in a while. Success is available to every athlete, to every team, and to every coach every single day. When we are about being a success, we also put ourselves in the best possible position to pick up those cherished wins as well. Unless, of course, we have a bad schedule!

*Build success!*

# How To Build Success

While success is available to each individual and to each athlete every day, it certainly does not come automatically or easily. It takes individuals who understand the process of being very effective, and who possess the characteristics that support and create such effectiveness. These characteristics are identifiable and can be developed in one's self or in others over time.

Through sport, coaches can nurture the development of these identifiable characteristics in the lives of their athletes. Six such characteristics (Hoffman, 1972) as originally identified by Robert Goodwin, soccer and track and field coach at St. Lawrence University, are proposed as appropriate goals for coaches to focus on developing within the athletes' sport experience. These characteristics are presented here and explained in light of the influence they have upon the educational value of athletics:

---

## FOUNDATIONAL BELIEFS

*"It Does Matter Whether You Win or Lose ... "*

- The development of the desire
to strive whole-heartedly toward excellence.

- The development of the realization
that nothing of any real value is ever achieved
without hard work and dedication.

- The development of a healthy attitude
toward competition.

- The development of a spirit
of cooperation.

- The development of self-confidence
through the use of one's own decision-making capabilities.

- The development of the desire
to have fun!

---

# The Development of the Desire to Strive Whole-Heartedly Toward Excellence.

Excellence! To strive toward excellence, where excellence is measured only against oneself, and never against another individual or against some predetermined standard or record. Literally, to strive to become the very best that one can become.

*And, however good that is, it is good enough!*

But the key word in this phrase is not excellence. Excellence is out there for all of us. But excellence will never come and find any of us. We must go and find and create our own excellence. No one ever finds that excellence without striving for it, and striving for excellence with all of their heart and emotion committed to finding excellence. And, no one ever strives for excellence or for anything else, without first being filled with the DESIRE to strive. The key word is *DESIRE*.

It is the goal, then, to develop the DESIRE to STRIVE whole-heartedly toward excellence, and. . .

## The Development of the Realization that Nothing of Any Real Value Is Ever Achieved Without Hard Work and Dedication

Again, we must not be distracted by typical coaching jargon. The focal words here are not hard work and dedication, but rather the words "real value." We have all been in situations where we have had the opportunity to achieve awards, sometimes in the form of trophies, medals, ribbons, plaques, certificates, rings, watches, jackets or pictures in the paper. In some of these situations, we haven't necessarily had to work very hard to gain our honor and award. Either the task wasn't that demanding, or we were more than talented enough to meet the demands, or possibly there just simply were more than enough awards to be presented and everyone or nearly everyone received one.

On the other hand, we also probably have each been in an achievement situation where gaining success and recognition did not come easily. We may have had to work very hard and be extremely persistent to even be in the competition. Maybe we weren't even successful the first time we attempted this task or direction. Possibly we failed repeatedly, and had to bounce back and become even better prepared. It might even be the case that when we did achieve success, there wasn't any tangible award presented to represent our achievement.

Which of these two situations brought us the greatest sense of pride and achievement? Which experience would we describe as being the most fulfilling and memorable? Quite assuredly, most would choose the latter. For it is in that investment of oneself, in the hard work and dedication that defines the commitment to the struggle, that we lay the groundwork for the great feelings of pride the we are then allowed to experience.

The medals, trophies, ribbons, and news clippings become tarnished, yellowed and worn with age. But the memories and sense of pride that we build as we invest ourselves in the acceptance of challenges and in the process of achieving live on in our memories, and even grow in value with time. This is REAL VALUE, and it can only be experienced if one first makes the personal investment of hard work and dedication.

It is our goal, to develop the realization that nothing of REAL VALUE is ever achieved without hard work and dedication, and. . .

## The Development of a Healthy Attitude Toward Competition

Quite frequently, those of us in sport are accused of being "too competitive." Many people are quick to perceive us negatively, and to proclaim their dislike for sport because it is just too competitive. They perceive sport, competition, and being competitive as negative and almost shameful.

This is unfortunate and often unfair. Competition is a fundamental and basic principle in American society. To take one's abilities and resources, and to work hard to build a better life for oneself and one's family is a fundamental right of all Americans. It is called free enterprise, and its hallmark is free and open competition.

In sport, society encourages athletes to learn how to be competitive and to succeed in a competitive environment. We are encouraged and expected to WIN! It is important to be the winner, and very often individuals are willing to do whatever it takes to achieve victory. Sometimes it becomes so important to win that "what it takes" may include cheating, unethical conduct, or even harming others who stand in the way of winning. And then, when victory is secured, and these individuals are proclaimed the winners, their fans also shower them with the accolade, "they're great competitors." They did what it took to win, even if it meant bending or breaking a few rules.

Maybe sport is too competitive. Maybe it has lost its way. Maybe the critics are correct. But it doesn't have to be.

A healthy attitude toward sport and competition recognizes that first, any athletic contest is no more than two or more individuals or teams competing against one another to determine who can do that activity best on that day. Even the Olympic Games themselves do nothing more than establish who performs best among those who compete on that day.

Too often our society has attached many extraneous and unnecessary meanings to an athletic victory. A victory does not crown an athlete champion for life. Similarly it does not guarantee anything about that athlete's opportunity for success in the very next competition. It merely establishes who did that thing best on that day. It really does not say anything about who has the best school or the best town. And, maybe most important of all, a win in the athletic arena does not determine who is the best person, but merely who won the race or the game.

Unfortunately, all of this extra baggage which we allow to become attached to winning in sport also adds to the participants' perceived urgency to gain the win, as well as the dreaded consequences of a loss. It is little wonder that ugly behaviors in the name of competition soon result. We must develop a healthy attitude toward competition, and with it. . .

## The Development of a Spirit of Cooperation.

Most individuals like to get things, and even work rather hard to identify the variables that will allow them to get what they desire. But when people are focused on getting something, and are about the business of trying to line up the variables which will get for them what they want, mostly what they actually get is FRUSTRATED! We just can't control all of these variables. We can't always control what we get, and so, we get frustrated. When we're frustrated, we often become quite ineffective, which in turn leads to more frustration.

But while we can't control all that we get, we have total control over all that we GIVE! We control what we give, to whom we give it, when we give it, how often we give it, and, above all, why we give it. When individuals are alert and sensitive to the needs of others, and respond unconditionally to help and meet those needs, then everyone wins. The ones in need win, because their needs have been met. The givers win, because they know that they have helped others in need, and are filled with joy and fulfillment.

In short, the givers gain the benefit of feeling great about themselves. Typically, when people feel great about themselves, they in turn are extremely effective at whatever it is that they do. As a result, by being more effective, these same individuals frequently find that they end up getting the very thing over which they had previously been so frustrated.

If given the choice to coach athletes who felt great about themselves or athletes who were frustrated and felt lousy about themselves, which would you pick? Most would choose to coach athletes who felt great about themselves.

A spirit of cooperation is all about caring, sharing and giving.

## The Development of Self-Confidence through the Use of One's Own Decision-Making Capabilities

Being self-confident and able to make decisions for oneself, about one-self and, above all, by one's self are skills just as are running, jumping, hitting, and throwing. Motor skills of sport are learned through instruction, modeling, trial, error, evaluation, correction, and repetition to allow for the learning of the desired skill to evolve through successive approximations.

Similarly, athletes learn to be confident of themselves in demanding and stressful sport settings as they are allowed to practice making decisions, particularly important decisions, by themselves. Coaches are often uncomfortable with this notion of athletes making key decisions, particularly in light of the reality that athletes are likely to make some poor decisions.

Ultimately, successful development and utilization of an athlete's capabilities in competitive performance is predicated on the individual's ability to make key decisions in crucial situations. For athletes to be confident of their own abilities to make important decisions, they must experience opportunities wherein their decision-making skills and self confidence are tested and allowed to grow.

## The Development of the Desire to Have Fun!

No one promises that sport will be fun. Nor, do we refer to the kind of "tee-hee, ha-ha, fool around" fun characteristic of locker rooms and team bus rides.

In this context, we speak of fun as the great sense of pride and satisfaction one has from finally mastering a skill after many long hours of practice, or the sense of completeness when one hits the 20-foot jumper—"SWISH"—all net, or the excitement experienced as a new personal record is achieved in the high jump—"and it felt so easy!" Yes, these are the feelings that all athletes and coaches know and are searching for!

*And, to have these feelings is FUN !!!*
*We speak here of the FUN of feeling great about oneself!*
*We speak of the FUN of feeling proud!*

And, when the athletes experience this FUN, invariably they are consumed with a desire to feel more of it again!

Developing the DESIRE to have FUN, then, may be the most important value coaches can ever teach. For when athletes are filled with this desire to have fun, they are likely to. . .

- be filled with the desire to strive whole-heartedly for excellence;

- realize that nothing of any real value is ever achieved without hard work and dedication;

- be great competitors, anxious to test their abilities, strategies and preparations against another, free from the fear of self-doubt of risking the loss of self-respect;

- gain greater personal strength from an attitude of respect, caring, sharing, giving and helpfulness towards others; and

- be willing to make those "tough" decisions when they count the most, confident that their preparations and committed investments will allow them to deliver the very best effort of which they are capable.

*Develop the DESIRE to have FUN!*

# Developing Your Own Foundational Beliefs

To identify and develop one's own personal foundational beliefs all coaches are challenged to consider and answer the questions which follow. To allow this process to be most effective, answers should be limited to three typewritten pages or less.

1. *What are the goals and purposes of athletics?*

*2. What are the ways and means of athletics?*

How do we go about accomplishing our goals and purposes? Specifically, how will we shape the athletic environment and what will this shaping allow athletes to experience, that will enhance the possibility that these goals and purposes will be accomplished?

It becomes obvious that for every goal in the answer to the first question, one must now match with it the means by which it can become accomplished.

*3. What is your philosophy of athletics?*

A philosophy is merely a personal statement of truth, of value and of what is important and real. While most coaches espouse a particular, unique philosophy, few have ever taken the time to develop, write, and verbalize their beliefs in a sequential and thorough process.

You may find this challenge to be inhibiting, even threatening. You may also find it to be enlightening, stimulating, refreshing and fulfilling.

*4. What are your foundational beliefs?*

Having now developed your philosophy, glean from it a few strong, positive statements capsuling the essence of your priorities, beliefs, and values regarding athletics and coaching. This may be the most important process or exercise you will ever experience as a coach.

## So What About Winning?

At the outset of this chapter we stated, "It Does Matter Whether You Win or Lose ...!" While there certainly is some importance and significance attached to whether or not we gain a win, we are all aware that it really does NOT matter much whether or not we win all of those games, matches, meets, tournaments, or races. Winning the next contest, or for that matter any contest, just cannot be that important.

But, without any question, it most certainly does matter that we

WIN, because it matters that we as coaches are WINNERS in the lives of each and every athlete with whom we have the opportunity to share the sport experience. For coaches, this must be the biggest and most important WIN of all! This is success!

Your own personal approach to Coaching Mental Excellence will be determined by your foundational beliefs. This foundation, together with your knowledge, understanding, and experience will determine the kind of athletic experience you provide for your athletes.

*Foundational Beliefs—Don't leave home without them!*

*Foundational Beliefs—Don't go to practice without them!*

*Coach, you really are someone special!*

## Acknowledgement

The authors gratefully acknowledge the influence and contribution of Mr. Robert Goodwin, longtime coach at St. Lawrence University, to the formulation and presentation of the concepts and ideas contained in this chapter. Coach Goodwin's personal example and deep personal commitment to model his beliefs and values in his daily approach to coaching athletes has provided positive influence on thousands of his athletes, and allowed the joy and magic of sport to live through them.

## References

Hoffman, Ronald (1972). "It does matter whether you win or lose . . .", *Scholastic Coach, 41.*

# Part II

# Team Dynamics

# Leadership and Team-Building

A popular perception among athletic coaches is that cohesion is an integral, if not indispensable, attribute of successful teams. Coaches should be aware of the relationships among their players if they want to create a winning team "chemistry." Understanding team dynamics is essential in developing effective team and individual performances.

In relating the importance of team dynamics to the success of an athletic team, Freischlag (1985) states:

> Team sport success is due largely to the individual abilities of the team members. However, developing a team by concentrating solely on the training of individuals is as inappropriate as trying to predict a team's performance by simply adding individual talents and comparing them to the opponents' talents. The missing element in such a prediction is team dynamics, the relationships within the group and with its coach, as they influence team performance (p. 67).

The theoretical framework regarding the group process in sport is addressed in a variety of sport psychology textbooks (Carron,1988; Cox,1990; Cratty,1989; Gill,1986; and LeUnes & Nation,1989) and is a performance-related issue often addressed by sport psychologists. The sport psychologist is often called upon to provide the coach with an educational perspective regarding team dynamics as well as with specific strategies for enhancing and facilitating the team-building process. In some cases the sport psychologist is also asked to help resolve intrateam conflicts. In this chapter, we review the following basic aspects of team cohesion as they operate in the sporting environment: the role of the coach in the team process; the coach's leadership style; the relationship between cohesion and team performance; and variables which influence team cohesion. In the course of this chapter, we will also specifically describe the formation of teams in an effort to assist coaches with the selection and implementation of appropriate team-building strategies.

## The Role Of The Coach In The Team Process

Coaches view team cohesion as the most critical challenge they face and for this reason the coach becomes the primary catalyst for developing and maintaining good team dynamics (Freischlag, 1985). Although coaching styles may vary, the following leadership formula is provided as a guide to effective athletic leadership:

$$Leadership\ =\ Integrity \times Communication \times \frac{Understanding}{of\ Human\ Behavior}$$

### Integrity

Paramount to the coach's leadership success is the development and maintenance of a trusting relationship with each player which ensures that individuals will be treated fairly. The coach's power as a leader is derived from two factors: position and trust. It is not enough to have the title "coach." The coach must earn the respect and loyalty of his or her players through honest and sincere daily interaction with them. He or she must also have a commitment to protect and preserve the rights of each player, presenting opportunities for personal growth in a cooperative and competitive environment.

## Communication

Leadership has been simply defined as the ability to influence others to do certain things (Murray, 1986). The coach is constantly communicating ideas to the athlete which will ideally result in a variety of sport-effective behaviors. The degree to which the athlete is receptive to the coaches' ideas is often determined by a variety of factors including: previous coach-athlete relationships; the coach's reputation; the decision-making style of the coach (authoritarian, dictatorial, democratic, or laissez-faire); and the credibility of the coach. A vital and mature coach-athlete relationship is based upon two-way communication, mutual trust, and respect.

The effectiveness of the coach-athlete communication process is sometimes threatened by the amount of administrative tasks the coach must perform as a part of his or her daily routine. Martens (1987) recognizes the importance of differentiating between leadership and management in the following statement:

> Leadership . . . is often confused with management. Management consists of planning, organizing, staffing and recruiting, scheduling, budgeting, and public relations. Leaders perform these functions, or delegate them to others, but they also do more. Leaders determine the direction for the future, and then marshal the resources within the organization to pursue that vision. Managers simply handle the routine, never questioning whether the routine should be done. This distinction is significant in sport, for too many teams are overmanaged and underled (p. 33).

Coaches and sport leaders should clearly understand the distinction between management and leadership and be constantly mindful of the adage: "You lead people and you manage things." A leader's vision is only ideological. It becomes real once it is clearly communicated to his or her followers through the process of "intellectual persuasion." The effectiveness of any sport group to achieve and realize their goals is dependent upon the athlete's ability to understand, accept, and actualize team philosophy, standards, norms, and goals.

### Understanding of Human Behavior

Effective leaders understand the dynamics which underlie human behaviors. Leaders have empathy and can relate compassionately with their followers, providing the support, encouragement and incentive necessary for personal improvement and self-actualization.

# The Coach's Leadership Style

The coach's ability to communicate and influence team members is directly related to his or her leadership style. Figure 3-1 illustrates the influence various leadership styles will have upon team communication and decision-making.

As a result of the demands involved in coaching athletic teams, the majority of coaches tend to adopt a task-oriented leadership style which is very purposeful and directive. Based on their review of research regarding the personality of the coach LeUnes and Nation (1989) state:

> When all is said and done, coaches are probably a bit authoritarian and conservative, but probably no more so than members of other professions. Too, being authoritarian is not all bad. At times, one firm hand has to be in control of things. The meetings between coaches and players at critical times in

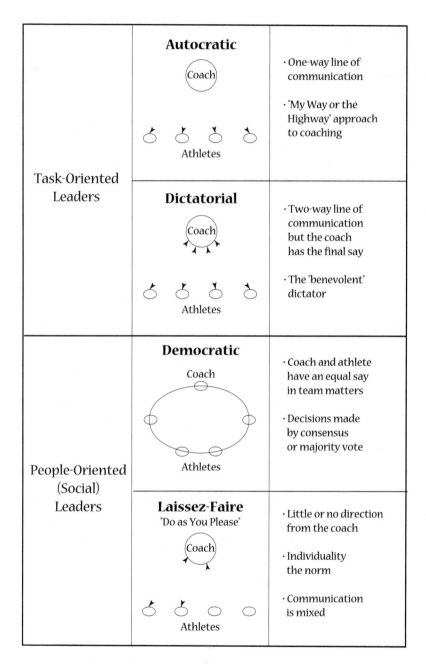

**Figure 3-1**    The influence of various athletic leadership styles on team communication and decision-making.

athletic contests call for someone taking control, and that person often is and should be the coach. Finally, coaches may be authoritarian or conservative in the job situation because it serves them well, but they may not be that way at all in dealings with others (pp. 398-399).

More experienced athletes have a preference for democratic behavior, coaching behavior which involves independent action, and stresses personal authority and independent decisions. These same athletes also prefer socially supportive coaching behaviors which demonstrate a concern on the coaches' part for the welfare of the individual athlete by emphasizing a positive team climate and warm interpersonal relationships (Carron,1988).

A democratic coaching style which provides for athlete participation in decisions pertaining to group goals, practice techniques, and game strategies and tactics, can provide the team members with a sense of "ownership" in the team, thus encouraging them to assume more of a personal investment and commitment to team goals (Carron, 1988; Weisen & Love, 1988).

Essentially the coach must be aware of the advantages and disadvantages between a task-oriented and a people-oriented leadership style. According to Cratty (1973, p. 231) a task-oriented leadership style is more advantageous because: it is more efficient with energy directed primarily toward the task; there is little time taken for interpersonal communication; the leader designates jobs quickly in highly-structured task situations; the leader is effective in situations highly favorable to leadership (i.e., high leader power and obvious task requirements); and the leader is effective in highly unfavorable situations (i.e., low leader power, unstructured task, or unaccepting group members).

Disadvantages of a task-oriented leadership style are that: it may raise anxiety levels of certain group members; it sacrifices the personal security of team members for expediency; it is less effective in moderately stressful situations in which group members may wish to interact; and it may not work well with important subordinates who have a need for secondary leadership.

Advantages of a people-oriented leadership style include: it may reduce anxiety in situations where the outcome was unfavorable; it can help the leader be more responsive to insecure people; it can help the leader deal better in situations that are moderately favorable for the leader and in which group members usually need a greater hand in decision making.

The disadvantages of a people-oriented leadership style include: there can be a lack of concern about successful execution of the task; the leader is less effective in highly stressful situations or those in which great power or power symbols are obviously awarded to the leader; and this style may cause anxious responses in group members who are highly task-oriented.

A word of caution is appropriate here for the coach who elects to use an autocratic leadership style which utilizes punishment to deter the performance mistakes and personal behaviors of their athletes. As Smith (1986) states: "... the quickest and most effective way to develop fear of failure is by punishing people when they fail." (p. 37) Aversive or negative reinforcement will tend to cause the athlete to play conservatively in an effort to avoid making mistakes. Such an attitude is detrimental to an athlete's performance because mistakes are an integral part of athletic participation and contests. The athlete who can be taught to accept and learn from their mistakes will, in the long run, be more effective since they are willing to accept challenges and utilize their skills in challenging and risky situations.

This is not to say that autocratic coaches are unsuccessful in the athletic world. Many task-oriented leaders are highly successful coaches primarily because they understand the delicate balance between positive and negative reinforcement in establishing leadership power and effectiveness. Essentially the leader's power and effectiveness is dependent upon: (1) how he or she uses authority, and (2) ability to gain the respect and trust of followers. Coaches can enhance their power by not only encouraging their athletes to strive for realistic and quality performance standards, but also by demonstrating a sincere concern for their athletes' welfare, both on and off the athletic field.

Finally, the coach must understand the team climate his or her leadership style will create in terms of: interpersonal relationships and communication with players; the team decision-making process; team and individual goals; understanding, acceptance and performance of player roles; acceptance of program standards and team rules; intrateam conflicts; and the overall enjoyment of the athletic experience.

In summarizing the relationship of coaching behavior to athlete preference and satisfaction, Carron (1988) summarized the results of research conducted with a variety of sport teams as follows:

1. Male athletes had a high preference for more training, and for autocratic and social support behavior from their coaches;

2. Female athletes had a high preference for more democratic behavior from their coaches;

3. As the coach's training and positive feedback increased, athlete satisfaction increased;

4. Coach–female athlete relationships were poor when the coach was perceived to provide less positive feedback and more autocratic behavior than was preferred.

# Understanding the Team-Building Process

Understanding the social dynamics of the group process is the coach's initial step toward effective team-building. This discussion will also focus on the role that the coach's philosophical view of his or her program plays in the process of team-building.

## Program Standards and Expectations

Coaches should have an established philosophy by which they conduct their program. These foundational beliefs are essential to an efficient athletic program and team. These principles should be in written form to allow for continual review by both coaches and athletes throughout the season.

The foundational beliefs of an athletic program represent the educational values, ideals, and standards upon which resulting attitudes and behaviors are predicated, evaluated, rewarded, and sanctioned. This is especially important when conflict arises within a team, since personal agendas and self-centered concerns can often lead to misinterpretation regarding the original mission and purpose of the team.

Furthermore, it is important for coaches to clearly differentiate between the educational mission and the purpose of their programs. The *educational mission* should be represented by several foundational belief statements which convey the program's philosophy. Examples of foundational belief statements presented in Chapter 2 which may represent the educational mission of an athletic program or team are:

- To develop the desire to strive whole-heartedly toward excellence.

- To develop the realization that nothing of any real value is ever achieved without hard work and dedication.

- To develop a healthy attitude toward competition.

- To develop a spirit of cooperation.

- To develop self-confidence through the use of one's own decision-making capabilities.

- To develop the desire to have fun.

On the other hand, *the purpose* of a particular athletic program or team can be defined in terms of outcome goals and objectives such as:

- To win each contest the team is involved in.

- To be the best team in the conference.

- To qualify for the state or national championships.

- To adhere to training rules and regulations.

- To prepare for competition by conscientiously attending and participating in practice sessions.

- For individual athletes to accept the responsibility to train in the "off-season."

Most sport leaders are well focused on the purposes of their programs but often lack a well-defined coaching philosophy which reflects their vision for the governance, conduct, and success of their teams. An ethically sound and educationally mature philosophy of sport and coaching, an essential ingredient of the team-building process is often missing.

## Team Dynamics

Once the educational philosophy of an athletic program is developed and clearly communicated by the coach, a team will progress through four stages in its development. These stages are: forming; storming; norming; and performing (Henschen & Richards 1986; Tuckman, 1965). This popular model has been used by sport psychologists to explain the group process in sport in an effort to enhance and facilitate the two most essential interrelated components of this process, namely, communication and productivity. Let us examine each of these stages as they relate to the performance effectiveness and team cohesion.

**Forming.** The initial, forming stage, the process of team selection, is a nervous time for the athlete. Their skills and talents are under close scrutiny and constant evaluation. This is a time of intense intrateam competition, personal anxiety and uncertainty for all players. Veteran players may perceive new recruits as a threat to their formerly secure positions on the team.

Once the team is selected it becomes essential for the coach to clarify and explain each player's role and responsibilities. Program standards and the philosophy, purpose, and mission of the program should also be clearly communicated and defined by the coaching staff.

It is also during this stage that team goals and individual goals are formulated. This can be accomplished in a variety of ways but the coach must decide whether goals are to be leader-formulated or team-formulated or whether the coaching staff and the team will share responsibility for formulated goals. It should be noted that if the team is involved in the formulation of team goals, they will be more likely to to behave in ways that will help them realize these goals.

It is also advisable for teams to set both *product* and *process* goals. Most teams are very concerned with product or outcome goals and neglect the process goals which have a considerable impact on players' enjoyment of the athletic experience. A common product or outcome goal of a team is to "win." A process goal which accompanies winning would be to become fit and healthy through participation in practice sessions.

Once team selection has taken place and roles and goals have been identified the team will begin to establish team social norms which will govern the behavior of the group members. A team identity is formed and a trusting team environment is established which stresses acceptance and sincere concern and care for teammates.

Belief in and commitment to the program standards and goals are expected to supersede individual performance goals during the forming stage, and cooperative behaviors (teamwork) are encouraged in an effort to attain team success. This is especially important in highly interactive and interdependent sports such as football, basketball, soccer, and volleyball.

**Storming.** A familiar quote which best describes this stage is: "A ship is safe in the harbor, but that's not what it's built for." Conflict is a natural and healthy part of the group process. Specific suggestions for dealing effectively with conflict (conflict resolution methods) will be presented later but the essential point is that conflict must be addressed and dealt with expeditiously and in accordance with previously established program standards and group norms. If not dealt with in this manner, conflicts and disagreements can rapidly erode team morale and cohesion.

Conflict within athletic teams usually results from the inability and unwillingness of certain individuals to accept their assigned roles or the team standards, norms, and goals. Other sources of team conflict are: athlete-athlete or coach-athlete miscommunication; misinterpretation of team policies; scoreboard mentality (emphasis on individual goals at the expense of teamwork and group success); over-exposure to the same individuals in an intense training, traveling, and competitive environment; and an intolerance of idiosyncrasies of team members.

Once conflict is resolved, the group or individuals involved recommits to the program standards and team goals. If not handled properly a team may remain in the storming stage and eventually become unproductive.

**Norming.** Once the group members have accepted their roles and understand the relationship of these roles to overall group performance the group can begin to function as a team. In this stage each member in the group fulfills the responsibilities of his or her assigned roles. Teamwork becomes evident in this stage as team members openly support and encourage each other.

**Performing.** This phase of team development is often referred to as the "flow stage." At this stage, accepted roles are maintained as the team artistically, creatively and effectively accomplishes its goals. There is an unspoken understanding between team members as well as between the coach and the team members.

The coach should take care to maintain this stage since a return to the storming stage would require that the rebuilding process begin anew.

# Cohesion And Team Performance

Team cohesion has been defined by Carron (1982) as "a dynamic process which is reflected in the tendency for a group to stick together and remain united in the pursuit of goals and objectives." (p. 124) Athletic teams may exhibit two specific dimensions of cohesiveness: task and social cohesion. *Task cohesion* involves members of a specific group working together to achieve a specific and identifiable task (Cox,1990), and *social cohesion* concerns whether members of a team like each other and enjoy each other's company (Cox, 1990).

In summarizing the influence of the various dimensions of cohesion upon team effectiveness Carron (1988) states:

> Cohesion in sport groups is made up of many elements—it is multidimensional in nature. And, each of these elements contributes in different ways to group interactions and group effectiveness. Social cohesion is the force that binds the group together into a socially harmonious unit. Undoubtedly, this has some relationship to performance effectiveness but the relationship isn't perfect. A team may be more pleasant when their isn't any conflict or tension but it isn't necessarily more productive. In the case of cohesion, as is the case with personality, it is necessary to determine what factor is important in the specific situation (p.160).

In her summary of the research literature regarding cohesiveness and performance in sport, Gill (1986, pp. 229-31) makes the following points:

1. Cohesiveness increases motivation and commitment to team goals, and hence cohesiveness should enhance performance; however, if emphasizing team goals detracts from the recognition and encouragement of individual contributions and goals, performance may suffer;

2. High social cohesion or interpersonal attraction could detract from performance if team members sacrifice performance goals and task interaction strategies to maintain friendship patterns. However, social support and encouragement from teammates have potential positive effects on performance if individuals are committed to performance and task goals;

3. Cohesiveness, defined and measured as attraction-to-group, is positively related to success in interactive sport teams;

4. Cohesiveness may influence performance, but the evidence indicates that success enhances cohesiveness and provides only weak indications that cohesiveness affects performance.

These findings regarding the relationship of cohesiveness to team performance would tend to suggest that: (1) the coach establish strong social intrateam cohesion in order to facilitate communication and cooperation among team members; and (2) that the primary emphasis of the team should be on task cohesion, that is, adherence to team and individual performance goals and behaviors.

## Variables Influencing Team Cohesion

Both the coach and sport psychologist need to constantly monitor and evaluate a variety of variables which can influence team cohesion. As identified by Cratty (1989) some of these variables are: stress, intrateam competition, member satisfaction, group size, stability of membership, communication characteristics, conformity and roles, and coalitions and cliques. Additional variables effecting team cohesion are: conflict resolution, intrastaff cohesion among the coaches; and the issue of playing time. Let us briefly address each of these variables and related issues.

## Stress

Although a moderate amount of stress created by competitions and pre-season training programs tends to bring team members together, too much stress can disrupt team cohesion. More specifically the physical and mental stress associated with training and performance demands should be closely monitored, especially when interpersonal conflicts and communication breakdowns occur.

## Intrateam competition

Intrateam competition for the purpose of team selection and to determine starting positions and playing time is an unavoidable reality of team sports and can often lead to conflict among athletes. In essence, excessive competition for recognition can prove detrimental to overall team performance (Cratty, 1989). Team members must be periodically rewarded for recognizing their roles, performing well, role performance, cooperative training and performance efforts, and recognizing the fact that the true success of the team is determined by *interteam* competition.

## Member Satisfaction

The concept of member satisfaction is probably best exemplified by the statement "nothing breeds success like success." Athletes like to be part of a successful program and team morale is usually high on winning teams. Conversely team morale can deteriorate on losing teams especially if preseason goals are not attained. For this reason, it is important that teams set process as well as product goals at the beginning of the season.

Team members may also become dissatisfied with training facilities and rehabilitative services, travel plans and scheduling, equipment, and the distribution of rewards.

## Group Size

There is usually an optimal group size for a given task. Essentially the size of the group should be no bigger or smaller than is necessary to effectively accomplish a task. All group members should be actively involved in such accomplishments. Problems related to team cohesion can arise in the athletic environment when certain team members don't get a chance to play. Many coaches over-recruit for their sport, and thus, many talented players may "sit the bench" though they practice regularly and energetically. On a basketball team only half out of 12 to 15 players may actually receive "playing time" on a regular basis. Faced with frustration and disillusionment regarding their opportunity to actually contribute to the team, the "reserve" player can feel isolated from the team as well as unmotivated.

## Stability of Membership

A stable team comprising a number of veterans who have successful association will tend to increase cohesion among all team members. And the more cohesive the team becomes, the less likely members are to choose to leave. It takes time for new group members to assimilate group norms and behaviors and if the new members of the group are in the majority a less cohesive team is often the result. In those cases, coaches must provide an atmosphere, via mentors, rookie camps, team social gatherings or "get-togethers," that effectively acquaints new members with the team's culture (Cratty, 1989).

## Communication Characteristics

The degree to which team members effectively communicate (verbally and non-verbally) with each other and their coach is often a reflection of team cohesiveness. The sport psychologist can be helpful in observing, categorizing, and evaluating team communication characteristics which may indicate individual communication problems such as: frequent disagreements and arguments; athlete-athlete or coach-athlete tensions; ineffective decision-making; unreceptivity to coaching; and uncommunicative, sullen, or reserved behavior. In general, cohesive teams are characterized by frequent, reciprocal, and positive verbal and non-verbal communications between group members (Cratty, 1989).

## Conformity and Roles

Perhaps the variable most affecting team cohesion is the ability of group members to conform to assigned roles. The sequential development of this process is role expectation, role clarity, role acceptance, and role performance. This is not always a smooth process for the coach to implement, and often extensive explanations and negotiations are required between the coach and athlete. In some cases a sport psychologist should be consulted. The success of highly interactive teams (i.e. basketball, football, volleyball) is often dependent upon the ability of team members to understand, accept, and excel in their assigned roles.

A helpful instrument for the coach or sport psychologist in assessing a team's role performance is the *Team Climate Questionnaire* (Carron, 1986).

## Coalitions and Cliques

Coalitions and cliques can be viewed as "teams within a team" and are most often formed on the basis of common opinions regarding team policies, goals, and leadership. These shared beliefs may either support the established goals of the team, thus enhancing team cohesion, or they may oppose team goals resulting in a decrease in team cohesion.

Coaches should be constantly aware of their teams' internal leadership and be willing to openly address issues of concern to team members. Constant communication with team members, especially the veterans, will provide the coach with the feedback necessary to address, clarify, and respond to specific team issues or conflicts which can effect team cohesion and performance.

## Conflict Resolution

Intrateam conflicts are a natural part of the team-building process in sport and usually stem from miscommunication and misinterpretation of team standards, norms, roles, and goals.

In order to minimize the potentially detrimental effect team conflicts can have upon cohesion, coaches should:

1. Speak to the team member(s) in a neutral setting away from the coach's office (i.e., go for a walk together, have lunch together, etc.);

2. Address conflicts directly, honestly, and expeditiously;

3. Listen to all sides of the issue/problem and then present your concerns;

4. Repeat the issue/problem until the emotional component has been diffused;

5. Relate the issue to team standards and goals so that the athletes can determine the effect of particular behaviors and attitudes upon team performance;

6. Negotiate a solution to the conflict/problem which is acceptable to all parties, thus facilitating a win-win outcome;

7. Have an objective party (i.e., athletic director, coach, sport psychologist, etc.) facilitate conflict resolution if necessary;

8. Explain to the athletes that conflict is healthy when dealt with in a mature, respectful, and open manner and that it can enhance understanding and communication among team members and the coach;

9. Use informal (conversation) or formal (meetings) follow-up sessions to evaluate the effectiveness of the established solution(s). Meet again to discuss the problem/issue if necessary.

## Intrastaff Cohesion

If we believe the adage: "The apple doesn't fall too far from the tree," it follows that unified leadership is an essential in cultivating and establishing a cohesive athletic team. The reality, however, is that among the members of many coaching staffs philosophical differences regarding the conduct of athletic programs do exist. Overly ambitious and eager assistant coaches often conflict with the head coach, but their concerns and opinions are seldom openly addressed.

Athletes can sense a "difference of opinion" among their leadership especially when they are coached by someone whose ideas and methods contradict the "status quo" for the existing team norms. Head coaches often require loyalty from their assistants to the established standards and norms which govern their programs. With so many responsibilities placed upon them, the last thing the head coach wants to do is "coach the coaches," in addition to coaching the athletes.

Coaching staffs should periodically spend extended periods of time together (i.e., a coaching retreat) to review and openly discuss team goals, standards, norms, training procedures, performance strategies, and individual coaching philosophies. Assistant coaches must clearly understand the role they are to play in the overall development of team talent. Job responsibilities resulting from these discussions, and in some cases negotiations, should be identified in writing in a further effort to clarify the roles of each member of the staff.

## Playing Time

Two of the most crucial issues related to team cohesion and member satisfaction are individuals' "playing time" and which players are selected to be the starters. Obviously, each player joined the team to test his or her abilities in the competitive setting and, to a lesser extent, in practice. Starters and players who receive a considerable amount of playing time receive more attention and more tangible rewards for their effectiveness.

The issue of playing time has a definite effect on coach-athlete communication since the athlete is well aware that the coach will decide who plays. For this reason, communication between the coach and athlete is often reserved, masked, inaccurate, or non-existent . Frustrated and disgruntled players can rapidly erode team cohesion, especially if their team is losing.

Coaches must do all that is possible to establish a trusting relationship with their athletes. Coach-athlete trust is developed when the coach demonstrates through word and action, sincere concern for each player on the team. The athlete will be more receptive to decisions which define their role on the team and determine their playing time if such care is demonstrated by the coach.

Disputes over playing time can result from players' *role expectations* developed while they were being recruited. The coach has an ethical responsibility to clearly and honestly project the role a recruit will play if he or she decides to become a member of the team.

Once the final selection of the team is made, the coach should then clearly define for each player what his or her role and responsibilities as a team member will be. Individual meetings with the head coach are necessary to address the issue of *role clarity* and will provide an atmosphere for *role negotiations* between coach and athlete. This is an ongoing process and is a prerequisite for *role acceptance* and *role performance* for the individual and the team.

The issue of playing time can also create a communication block between the athlete and sport psychologist if the athlete doesn't feel their discussions are kept confidential. Naturally, the coach will be interested in how the sport psychologist is helping the athlete explore and cope with problems such as playing time. The coach and sport psychologist must also trust each other and the coach must believe that the sport psychologist is helping the athlete deal with team and personal issues in light of the established team standards, norms, and goals.

# Principles Of Leadership and Team-Building

Leadership is at the core of the athletic experience. As stated previously in this book, "the athlete meets sport at the coach." The quality and effectiveness of participation in the athletic experience is dependent upon the ability of the athletic administrator and coach to effectively guide his or her athletes through the challenges and rigors of competition and training.

The following principles summarize the concepts presented in this chapter and provide guidelines for conducting a sound, effective, and educational athletic program:

1. *Leadership = Integrity × Communication × Understanding of Human Behavior.* Integrity and sound foundational beliefs regarding the value of sport as an educational process of personal growth are essential ingredients in leadership effectiveness. The coach's challenge, then, is to provide athletes with opportunities that are appropriate for their athletic and personal development.

2. *Athletic excellence with integrity.* The ability of the coach to understand and adhere to the long range vision of his or her philosophy of sport will certainly be tested by his or her desire to

win. By emphasizing a process orientation to sport the coach can overcome "scoreboard mentality" and keep a healthy perspective on the demands and pressures of the athletic environment. A process orientation focuses on attaining victory with honor.

3. *Know your leadership style.* Be aware of the implications, strengths, and weaknesses of autocratic, dictatorial, democratic, and laissez-faire coaching styles. Your style will be instrumental in communicating the values and performance goals of your program. Your actions will mirror your beliefs about sport and athletic achievement. The coach's power derives from trust. Can the athlete in your program feel secure that you are acting on behalf of his or her personal welfare?

4. *Athletes have a preference for autocratic coaching styles.* As a result of their socialization athletes expect an autocratic or dictatorial coaching style. If you elect to lead in this manner, emphasize intellectual persuasion and reason rather than fear. Spend time with your players outside of practice and competition to demonstrate your concern for their welfare.

5. *Recognize gender differences as they relate to your coaching style.* Whereas male athletes will prefer more autocratic and task-oriented coaching styles, female athletes tend to prefer more democratic and socially oriented coaching styles. Research has found that coach-female athlete relationships were poor when the coach was perceived to provide less positive feedback and to exhibit more autocratic behavior than was preferred (Carron, 1988).

6. *Understand the team building process.* Recognizing and anticipating the "natural" stages (i.e., forming, storming, norming, and performing) your team will experience throughout the season will enhance your coaching effectiveness. Coaches must be able to resolve conflict expediently throughout this process.

7. *Success enhances team unity or cohesion.* A common misperception is that a socially cohesive team will be a winning team. Your team will become more cohesive as it successfully accomplishes its goals. Focusing on the development and realization of task cohesion will develop a sense of pride and mastery among team members. Team and individual goals must be challenging but realistic in order to nurture and develop this process.

8. *Social cohesion is very desirable for highly interactive sports.* Mutual support, friendships, and encouragement among teammates can positively effect performance if the athletes are committed to performance and task goals. High social cohesion within teams is necessary to promote the willingness of team members to "work together" to achieve team goals.

9. *Be sensitive to the life cycle of your team.* Be aware that the athletic environment can affect team unity and performance. Environmental factors that may be operating include: training and performance-related stress; intrateam competition; member satisfaction; team size; stability of team membership; the team's communication characteristics; role conformity; coalitions and cliques; conflict resolution; intrastaff cohesion; and playing time.

## References

Carron, A. V. (1982). Cohesiveness in sport groups. *Journal of Sport Psychology, 4,* 123-138.

Carron, A. V. (1986). The sport team as an effective group. In J. M. Williams (Ed.), *Applied Sport Psychology: Personal Growth to Peak Performance* (pp. 93-105). Mountain View, CA: Mayfield.

Carron, A. V. (1988). *Group dynamics in sport: theoretical and practical issues.* London, Ontario: Spodym Publishers.

Cox, R. H. (1990). *Sport psychology: concepts and applications* (2nd ed.). Dubuque, IA: Wm. C. Brown.

Cratty, B. J. (1989). *Psychology in contemporary sport* (3rd ed.), Englewood Cliffs, NJ: Prentice-Hall.

Freischlag, J. (1985). Team dynamics: implications for coaching. *Journal of Physical Education, Recreation and Dance, 56,* 67- 71.

Gill, D. L. (1986). *The psychological dynamics of sport.* Champaign, Illinois: Human Kinetics.

Henschen, K. P., & Richards, E. D. (1986) *Forming, storming, norming and performing: group development stages in sport.* An unpublished paper, University of Utah, Salt Lake City.

LeUnes, A. D., & Nation, J. R. (1989). *Sport psychology: An introduction.* Chicago: Nelson-Hall.

Martens, R. (1987). *Coaches guide to sport psychology.* Champaign, Illinois: Human Kinetics.

Murray, M. (1986). Leadership effectiveness. In J. M. Williams (Ed.),

*Applied Sport Psychology: Personal Growth to Peak Performance* (pp. 93-105). Mountain View, CA: Mayfield.

Tuckman, B. W. (1965). Developmental sequence in small groups. *Psychological Bulletin.* 63, 384-399.

Weisen, K. , & Love, P. (1988). Who owns your team. *Strategies,* 2, 5-8.

# Part III

# The Psychology of Coaching

# Effective Motivation

Motivation is the fuel for an athlete's performance. It cannot be seen; it *can* be felt by a competitor. It is intangible, but the athlete is keenly aware whether it is present or absent. Just as certain fuels burn hotter than others, motivation has varying levels of intensity and efficiency.

Performance is directly related to the intensity of motivation. An athlete who is intensely motivated to perform well, is much more likely to succeed. Indeed, motivation is often called the great equalizer in sport.

Though people frequently use the terms motivation and arousal to mean the same thing, they are different. Arousal, which will be discussed in the next chapter, is the physiological response to a stimulus. Motivation, on the other hand, is the psychological force that drives us to perform well. It is the direction and intensity of purpose. Having a sense of purpose causes an athlete to pursue a sport. The athlete's purpose often derives from the pleasure of participating in the sport, the satisfaction of accomplishing a task, and the admiration he or she earns from others as a result of participation in the sport. In other words, the athlete has his or her own particular reason for performing. This reason is what motivates the athlete.

Levels of motivation differ among athletes. Each athlete pursues different goals with varying degrees of intensity. Consider the first part of motivation—direction. Some athletes are motivated by success, while others are motivated by a fear of failure. Athletes also vary in their intensity levels, ranging from very low to extremely intense. Intensity, the second element of motivation, in essence has to do with the amount of "control" an athlete feels over the situation.

Why athletes vary in their sense of direction and intensity can be illustrated in the following "motivational patterns." These patterns can operate together in varying combinations. Examining them in sequence and in some detail will help us understand an athlete's behavior. These patterns are of special importance to those involved in sport, as they represent an athlete's typical motivational concerns.

# Patterns of Athletic Motivation

## Learned Helplessness

A common motivational pattern in young athletes is "learned helplessness". This pattern is exhibited by a lack of effort and is characterized by low intensity behavior in practice and in competition. Athletes who fall into this pattern of behavior attribute success and failure to external factors such as luck or an opponent's superior ability. Therefore, this athlete believes that no matter how hard he or she tries, the outcome is largely beyond his or her control. Most likely, this pattern was *learned* in early sporting experiences, through participating on consistently losing teams or competing against unfair opponents. These experiences contribute to a feeling of helplessness and can easily arise during youth sports when athlete's physical maturation levels vary greatly.

Because this is a learned motivational pattern, it can be unlearned and the athlete can be retrained to adopt a "learned effective" motivational pattern (Rotella, 1981). The learned effective athlete is intensely motivated and attributes success and failure to internal factors such as *effort, ability, and skill.* The learned effective athlete believes that the outcome of competition is, for the most part, within his or her control. Learned effectiveness will be described in detail later in this chapter.

The learned helpless athlete must be taught to redefine success and to measure improvement against one's self, rather than against another. The coach can help in this by keeping a performance chart for an athlete and by encouraging him or her to focus on self-improvement. The desired outcome is a newfound sense of control. Competition with others helps push an athlete to excel but should not be considered the ultimate measure of success. An athlete can only control his or her performance. An athlete has no control over an opponent's ability, preparation, effort, or motivation.

The learned helpless athlete needs to experience success and improvement. Setting short term goals and accomplishing them is very important. It is also helpful if the athlete experiences some sort of success in daily practice to gain confidence and a sense of control.

### Coaching the "Learned Helpless" Athlete

1. *Redefine success*—success equals improvement in one's own performance.
2. *Chart performance and improvement.*
3. *Develop short term goals*—Point to small successes.
4. *Arrange for the athlete to experience some success in daily practice sessions.*
5. *Help the athlete to feel that he or she has earned success.*

## Fear of Failure

A second motivational pattern involves the athlete's tendency to pursue success or to avoid failure. When an athlete's primary goal is to pursue success he or she is said to be positively motivated. Conversely, for negatively motivated athletes the primary goal is to avoid failure. A preoccupation with avoiding failure is emotionally draining for athletes. This attitude takes the fun out of sport and has been reported to be the primary motivational factor among young athletes. This "fear of failure," though a strong motivator, can cause performance problems. Any time there is fear, there is over-anxiousness, which contributes to poor performance.

Fear of failure is caused by a number of different factors. It can stem from the exercise of conditional love or the inappropriate use of rewards by a parent or coach. It can also evolve if the athlete has acquired a habit of deriving his or her self-worth from winning and losing. Fear of failure can also result from never having failed. Some gifted athletes have succeeded all their lives and are ill-prepared for a new level of competition where losing is a real possibility.

The symptoms of fear of failure include: making up excuses for lackluster performance before or after competition, worrying about what others will think of a poor performance, and preoccupation with the opponent's reputation or ranking. An athlete who operates under fear of failure is indecisive about strategy and perceives that he or she has no control. These feelings are caused by over-anxiousness and a lack of appropriate concentration.

For athletes with this pattern, failure is a measure of their self-worth and a rational and constructive analysis of a loss is lacking. Therefore, the athlete makes excuses for losing and may even develop psychosomatic ailments prior to or during competition.

The initial step in dealing with this issue is for the athlete to acknowledge that a fear of failure exists. The coach can help this type of athlete through careful and patient communication after a win or loss. It must be emphasized that winning or losing has little to do with self-worth and that, in fact, a loss can have a positive effect by serving to point out weaknesses. A loss also teaches the athlete the importance of persistence, patience, and believing in one's self through adversity—qualities of all great athletes.

In an eight-lane race there is the potential for eight runners to set personal records, yet the fear-of-failure athlete emphasizes that there will be seven losers. As with the learned-helpless athlete, the coach must help this athlete redefine success as competition against one's self, not as out-performing those in the other seven lanes.

### Coaching the "Fear-of-Failure" Athlete

1. *Separate the athlete's identity from his or her performance.* Communicate approval for the athlete after both winning and losing performances.

2. *Encourage athletes to learn from a loss.* Losing can be a valuable part of the athlete's development since it can: point out weaknesses to improve upon; teach patience; teach persistence; develop belief in one's self through adversity.

3. *Success = effort × ability × preparation × will.*

4. *Employ goal setting techniques which emphasize process and personal goals.*

## Fear of Success

Fear of success can be defined as a preoccupation with the *perceived* negative aspects of winning. An athlete who has a fear of success is typically overwhelmed, not by success but by the "excess baggage" that it brings. Several of the main causes for this motivational pattern include having to deal with fans' unrealistic expectations, having the competition constantly "gunning" for you, having the responsibility of being a role model because of the added visibility of being number 1, and experiencing teammates who become jealous or envious of your success.

This type of athlete may be said to have a narrow comfort zone.

The athlete is comfortable in the number 2 or 3 spot but would rather not make the transition required to become number 1. Mental barriers arise and the athlete finds ways to avoid competition. He or she may even let up during a game. It is likely that these athletes have been physically trained for success, but have failed to prepare for outside challenges.

There are several strategies to combat fear of success. First, the athlete must focus on his or her goals. It is imperative that the athlete adhere to these goals rather than allow fans to impose expectations on him or her. The fans and media have a way of causing one's focus to become tainted and skewed. Having a well-structured goal setting program with a blueprint for success will help an athlete adjust to success and failure. It is important that the coach help the athlete stay in touch with his or her goals.

A coach can prepare an athlete for success by suggesting constructive approaches to the anticipated "baggage" success will bring. Simply having a "talk" in which the coach and athlete discuss solutions can alleviate the fears associated with success. When individuals feel that they have some control over the anticipated situation then they can approach it with confidence. In short, developing strategies for dealing with outside influences and pressures can diffuse fears of success, permitting the athlete to confidently pursue excellence.

Helping the athlete to expand his or her comfort zone is another factor in overcoming the fear of success. Athletes can use positive visualization techniques to pre-image themselves performing successfully in competitive situations. Some athletes aren't accustomed to seeing themselves at their best. They have always had idols to look up to who were the best. So, becoming an idol or role model for others disrupts their perception of things. Mastery rehearsal techniques, those discussed in chapter 6, can facilitate a reorientation that will allow the athlete to see himself or herself in a new light.

It is also important to be aware of the team dynamics. When one individual is more successful than other team members, social alienation can creep in. It is extremely important for the coach to immediately diffuse this conflict. Teammates may become jealous or envious of the attention being heaped on the star, who probably didn't ask for all of the attention. This attention may cause the star athlete to feel uncomfortable and alienated from the team. It may even lead to a fear of success. If the situation isn't addressed expeditiously, the athlete may begin to let up during competition in an effort to resolve his or her discomfort and become a "normal" athlete again.

### Coaching the "Fear of Success" Athlete

1. *Help the athlete adhere to his or her personal goals*, and to put the fans' expectations in perspective.

2. *Anticipate and prepare for being #1.*

3. *Expand the athlete's comfort zone*—encourage the athlete to "picture" him- or herself as the best:

    *"Fake it 'till you make it!"*

4. *Encourage the athlete to play his or her own game.*

5. *Differentiate between the athlete's "identity" and success.*

# Perfectionist

The next motivational pattern, which is closely related to the fear-of-failure pattern, describes the perfectionist. At first glance, the perfectionist is the ideal athlete. This athlete works very hard, has high expectations, and an intensity that is unsurpassed. But ironically, it is these qualities which become a hindrance. Like the fear-of-failure athlete, this athlete equates self-image with performance. This correlation drives the perfectionist's behavior. The athlete cannot enjoy success and is never satisfied with his or her performance.

When expectations are great, excess pressure and stress are placed upon the athlete who, in turn, works harder, longer, and more intensely. He or she feels guilty about resting or being light-hearted. The belief that hard work always leads to success fails to hold up under these conditions as physical and mental fatigue creep in, and the athlete reaches the point of diminishing returns. At this point the perfectionist responds in the only way he or she knows how. The athlete again works harder, longer, and more intensely, which only intensifies his or her feelings of frustration and hopelessness.

The coach must help the athlete with the mentality to put performance into perspective. One must impress upon this athlete that mental and physical rest is both important and positive. Remember, *the challenge for this athlete is not the hard work; the challenge is making room for rest.* This athlete must be encouraged to take time to enjoy the positive aspects of each performance. This can be done by encouraging the perfectionist to verbalize the satisfying aspects of the experience following the event. Initially, it will take a lot of effort to get him or her to be expressive and positive. This athlete should also be encouraged to dwell more on the *pleasure of performing* (the process) than on the adulation or rejection that typically result from winning or losing (the product). Since the perfectionist is often consumed by the long vision, he or she can also benefit from visual reminders, such as progress charts, which show how far he or she has come and the improvement he or she has made.

## Coaching the "Perfectionist" Athlete

1. *Develop a positive association with mental/physical rest.*

2. *Encourage the athlete to take time to enjoy success.*

3. *Encourage verbal communication* about satisfying aspects of performance. The coach must ask for and then listen to the athlete's perspective.

4. *Dwell on pleasure of process* rather than outcome.

5. *Enjoy the process of achieving goals—enjoy getting there!* Use visual reminders of the athlete's progress—charts, etc.

6. *Help athletes to avoid overworking at their sport* by providing a balanced and realistic time-orientation to their training.

## Under-Achiever

At the other end of the continuum is the motivational pattern of the under-achiever. The under-achiever can be described as a "natural athlete" because he or she possesses great talent and has enjoyed great success without hard work or self-discipline. Ironically, this athlete's greatest competition is his or her own natural talent. The under-achiever has no appreciation for hard work and feels no pride when effort translates into success. This athlete tends to dwell on past successes, believing that the future will naturally be filled with the same success. Typically, this athlete will reach a level of competition for which he or she is unprepared. The under-achiever will fail before he or she realizes his or her potential because of a lack of positive work habits.

The coach should encourage this athlete not to give up, but to change. Most importantly, the under-achiever athlete must understand that there is no quick-fix or magical solution for this predicament. This athlete must demonstrate a commitment to change and the commitment should be verbalized.

The under-achiever must then be educated about the relationship between effort and success. This can be achieved by setting short term goals and pursuing them with intense effort and concentration. The athlete must be made to see that exerting effort promotes feelings of pride and a desire to reach his or her potential. By setting goals this athlete learns to focus on the future, understanding that past success does not insure future success. He or she learns that success comes from having a good attitude, sound goals, and dedication. Whereas the perfectionist places too much emphasis on the *future*, the under-achiever is focused on the *past*. Again, it is important for the underachiever to focus on self-improvement and to be aware that his or her greatest competition is against himself or herself.

### Coaching the "Under-Achieving" Athlete

1. *Obtain a verbal commitment from athlete to change.*

2. *Educate athletes about the effort—success ratio:* Chart progress. Set goals.

4. *Expand time orientation to include past, present, future.*

5. *Stress that he or she competes against one's self*—Stress self-improvement.

## Learned Effectiveness

The ideal motivational pattern can be described as "learned effectiveness," a term coined by Rotella (1981). This athlete perceives and reacts to sport in ways that will maximize effectiveness. This athlete assumes control and never blames others or makes excuses for failure. Weaknesses are seen as challenges to be met head-on. This athlete has a strong emotion of pride and understands the feeling of accomplishing a goal through hard work, patience, and persistence. This athlete's confidence, based on a lifetime of work, cannot be shattered through a single, poor performance. He or she is set up for success by proper preparation and goal setting. He or she also knows that external factors such as size, strength, or personality do not *alone* determine success. Rather it is the internal attributes, such as determination, will, and commitment which will make an athlete successful.

This athlete has also enjoyed success in the past, and gaining confidence from accomplishing goals. He or she is motivated by aspirations and remains focused on goals, having the ability to block out distracting thoughts during his or her performance.

## Characteristics of the "Learned Effective" Athlete

- Makes no excuses, lays no blame.

- Accepts responsibility for minor losses.

- Sees weaknesses as challenges.

- Strong emotion of pride.

- Confidence based on preparation.

- Sets performance, process, and personal goals. Goals are the *ends*, well-structured plans are the *means*.

- Determines success by internal factors.

- Acknowledges significance of past, present, and future.

In this chapter we have demonstrated that an athlete's motivational pattern can have a great effect on his or her approach to sport. Unproductive motivational behavior can be recognized, understood and corrected. As we involve ourselves in the lives of athletes, we must take the time to analyze motivational perspectives and to help athletes reach their potential through the use of effective motivation.

## References

Rotella, R. (1981). "Learned helplessness: A model for maximizing potential", Bunker, L. and Rotella, R., (Eds.), *Sport Psychology: Psychological Considerations in Maximizing Sport Performance*, University of Virginia , HPER Dept. Press.

5

# The Composition of Confidence

Anxiety may be the most overemphasized topic in the field of sport psychology. Athletes are taught how to avoid anxiety, how to alleviate anxiety, how to block out anxious thoughts, how to detect over- anxiousness, how to... etc., etc. By focusing on how to avoid anxiety we risk causing many athletes to become fixated on the problem. By belaboring the problem we inadvertently teach the athlete avoidance rather than pursuance.

One could argue that confidence is at the opposite end of the continuum from anxiety. Assuming this is an accurate perception, our goal should be to have our athletes pursuing confidence rather than avoiding anxiety. In other words, we want our athletes pursuing success rather than avoiding failure.

As our athletes seek to build confidence they move away from anxiety. Therefore, as an athlete develops skills and techniques which enhance his or her confidence, anxiety becomes less and less of a factor.

Confidence is simply a choice. For an athlete to gain confidence the word volition must be understood. Volition can be defined as "the will to choose." Volition has a spectrum which goes something like this:

> **"I won't."**
>      **"I can't."**
>           **"I'd like to."**
>                **"I'll try."**
>                     **"I can."**
>                          **"I commit."**

To achieve excellence in sport there is but one choice to be made. By choosing the attitude of "I commit," an athlete puts himself or herself in position to succeed. We have no guarantees of success, but when the athlete commits to an objective, the probability of reaching it is enhanced. The attitude of "I'll try" leaves the athlete susceptible to doubt.

It has been said that the greatest power in the world is the power to choose. Each person wakes up in the morning confronting an array of choices. The choices they make will dictate their confidence level. Gary Player, professional golfer, says it best, "Every morning I have a choice, I simply choose to be positive."

When we asked athletes to recall a time when they felt very confident before competing, the following list of reasons was given:

- Recent success

- Good week of practice

- Like the site of competition

- Weather was in their favor

- Positive comment from coach or friend prior to competing

- Played well here the year before

- Great warm up

- Liked lane assignment, playing partners, or seeding

This list of sources of confidence includes few factors that athletes can control. These responses demonstrate that many athletes derive their confidence from external factors. To illustrate the point further we asked these same athletes to picture the following scenario:

> You are at a competition in which you performed poorly last year, you are coming off a poor performance and have had a bad week of practice. You don't like the place of competition and the weather is not what you had hoped for. During warm-up someone questioned your skill and your coach yelled at you. *Can you be confident in that situation?*

The athletes just laughed and said not likely. That is understandable if one's confidence is based on external factors. However if one's confidence is based on internal factors, it is possible for an individual to feel confident despite unfavorable external factors. Furthermore, when confidence is internally-based, the athlete has a greater sense of control. As will be discussed later, control is a major factor in motivation.

The question to be answered, then, is how to develop internal confidence. There are five elements of confidence:

- Belief in Method

- Positive Self-Talk

- Positive Visualization

- Trust

- Mapmaking

Central to each of these elements is the notion of volition—*the will to choose.*

# Belief In Method

The first choice athletes must make is to believe in their method. In most sports today there is more than one right way to hit, swing, kick, vault, jump, etc. There is more than one training program that will lead to success. Conditioning programs are many and varied, and with all the choices these variables present, it becomes clear that the critical choice is not the method chosen, but *believing* in the method chosen.

Therefore, the first choice an athlete must make in pursuit of confidence is to understand and believe in his or her training procedures and techniques. The days of blind allegiance have passed. There is so much information written about technique, training, etc., that we must educate athletes as to why a particular method is best for them. We must take the time to emphasize for the athlete that believing in one's method is the first step toward confidence.

# Positive Self-Talk

The second element which enhances confidence is self-talk. As human beings we are constantly in dialogue with ourselves. The human brain communicates to the body through words and pictures. No voluntary action takes place without a preceding thought. Therefore, performance of any kind is preceded by self-talk.

It has been said that the most intimate and influential messages come from what we say to ourselves. Because this is so and because performance is initiated by self-talk it becomes very apparent that controlling self-talk is essential to a positive performance. It is also apparent that if our self-talk is negative our performance will suffer.

Positive self-talk is nothing more than being our own best friend. Our communication with troubled close friends is very positive and encouraging regarding their talent. We reach out to them reminding them that they still have the talent. We remind them of their great performances in the past and point to their strengths. In short, we attempt to steer their thinking from pessimism to optimism.

Now, to bring this closer to home, think back to a time when you were in the midst of a terrible slump, when everything seemed to be against you. Can you recall your self-talk? If you are like most people your self-talk did not resemble the communication that you gave to your friends. During slumps, failures, losses, it is easy to beat up on ourselves through negative, self-defeating criticism. This is all the more true for our athletes.

Self-talk represents a choice. There is nothing inside the brain forcing negative thoughts. Negative self-talk stems from our reaction to the circumstances. Therefore, the athlete must choose positive self-talk, the second building block of confidence.

## Positive Visualization

Thirdly, the athlete must choose to visualize success. In the context of sport, visualization is nothing more than picturing the performance before the event takes place. The term may be shrouded in mystery because its been overused. We need to remove the mystery and provide a practical rationale for using visualization.

It has been said that we cannot become what we cannot see ourselves becoming. We have also heard the term, "what you see is what you get." Both of these are truisms. The pictures that we carry in our mind's eye have a great impact on our motor responses. Our eyes (or mind's eye) relay vital information to the muscles. This information is turned into "feel" which is the cornerstone to performance.

For example, visualizing the freethrow moving through the air with perfect rotation and trajectory and then falling gently through the hoop will set the shooter's "feel" in motion. The perfect technique will then become more natural or automatic for the shooter. In the same vein, if the shooter is visualizing a "brick shot" (because of fear of producing that shot) the muscles are being pre-set to lay a brick.

Athletes can utilize visualization to improve performance in a couple of ways. Visualization can be effectively employed before an upcoming game. The athlete sets his or her mind for success by envisioning an effective performance. The athlete shows up for the competition expecting success. Such positive visualization fills the athlete with confidence rather than doubt or fear.

Athletes can also use visualization techniques during competition. The purpose here is to set the mind up for success at the moment of performance, remembering the influences of positive imagery.

The pictures in our mind's eye are images that we choose, either consciously or sub-consciously. To maximize potential, these pictures must be chosen carefully. Visualization is not a gimmick but a valid method for improving athletic performance. One can only arrive at an athletic contest with confidence when an athlete has chosen to create images of success.

## Trust

The fourth choice that an athlete must make is to trust rather than doubt. This element of confidence-building requires that the athlete says "I commit." This is the key to unlocking the athlete's potential.

Each person is blessed with potential. There are three things we know about potential. First, no one has ever reached his or her potential. Secondly, we can't predict potential. And third we do not know what our potential is. However, *trust in preparation, ability, and strategy* is intricately intertwined with potential. We know that if one performs with trust, he or she is more likely to reach his or her potential. We also know that doubt inhibits potential and in fact can lock potential inside. This can be witnessed every day as talented athletes spiral into a slump, locking their potential inside. For these athletes, talent is present, trust is lacking.

Trust doesn't guarantee success but it does create an environment that fosters success. Trust is the opposite of doubt, worry, and fear. Trust gets the athlete in the right frame of mind to perform. In fact, trust predisposes the athlete to perform well and then allows nature (talent) to take over.

Trust is a mindset. It is not dependent on circumstances or situations. It is a matter of volition—the will to choose.

# Mapmaking

The fifth choice an athlete must make to ensure confidence concerns goal setting. Everyone seems to talk about the merits of goal setting. Research has proven that goal-setters perform better. Most coaches set team and individual goals with their athletes. However, an athlete's confidence is not enhanced by the mere identification of goals. The goal setting process must become a "mapmaking" or "blueprinting" procedure in which goal attainment is the focus.

If a person's goal is to drive from Los Angeles to New York City, the goal has been identified. However, just establishing the goal does not accomplish the goal. The missing ingredient is the map. The goal represents the person's dream, the map is the vehicle for making the dream a reality. Without a blueprint for success many goals will become lost dreams. Having a map to follow enhances confidence by plotting the athlete's progress. It also increases an athlete's expectations for further achievement. As a result, the athlete approaches competition with confidence.

Careful study of blueprints for success reveals that there may be several different courses which may lead to success. Choosing a specific blueprint helps the athlete to focus and be committed to the goal. It also gives the athlete a feeling of control because improvement can be measured against a concrete plan. A well-structured goal setting program based upon a specific blueprint is essential if an athlete is to approach an athletic contest with confidence.

## Guidelines for Effective Goal Setting

- *Set goals which focus on the process rather than the outcome.* Long term goals are attained by following a blueprint.

- *Emphasize improvement of one's performance.* Goals should then be established by this individualized standard. For example, instead of aiming to finish in the top three places in a race, set a goal of improving one's time and racing strategies. The athlete can control his or her time. He or she cannot control all of the variables that affect place. Focusing on running an appropriate pace and employing certain race strategies will engage the athlete in a process which will enable them to place as high as possible. Remember, control is directly related to motivation.

- *Don't try to do too much too soon.* Perfectionists tend to develop elaborate goal setting programs which can become exhausting and self defeating.

- *Goals should be flexible. Goal setting is an art which takes time to perfect.* There are many unforeseen occurrences in sport which require adjustment. Constant evaluation and adjustment are part of the goal setting process and should be seen as healthy, not problematic. Long term goals are nothing more than dreams which are constantly evolving.

- *Long term goals should be supported by both intermediate and short term goals.* Each new stage of accomplishment should be rewarded. Stopping to "smell the roses" is healthy and can motivate the athlete to achieve new heights and stay fresh. Deriving satisfaction and pleasure along the journey helps to prevent burnout and encourages us to experience life rather than to let it pass us by.

- *Have your athletes write down their goals.* Next, have them substantiate their goals with a map for success. Keep these on file. Accountability is another great motivator and having a record gives you a window into the life of your athlete.

- *Have your athletes set goals outside of sport as well.* This shows that you think of them as whole people, not just athletes. Being a whole person increases the chances of success on the athletic field. Coach the person first, the sport second.

In conclusion, it is clear that coaches would do well to help athletes understand the factors that comprise confidence. Confidence is a choice. It is important that coaches help athletes understand what the choices are. An athlete must choose to believe in his or her method, choose positive self-talk, choose positive visualization, choose to trust rather than doubt themselves, and choose to be a mapmaker. None of these choices is dependent on outside factors. Each depends on the athlete's will to choose.

# Creative
# Concentration

For years athletes have heard coaches repeat the words, "Come on now, concentrate, keep your head in the game!" Most likely, it was never really explained what was meant by the word "concentrate." We always assumed that an athlete knew exactly how to concentrate and how to turn the concentration switch on and off.

Concentration is not interpreted in the same way by each athlete. It cannot be easily described as it is composed of different phases. Basically, concentration is the focus of attention. This focus can be directed externally or internally. The athlete can be concentrating on the cross bar, runway, wind direction, crowd, or opponents, all external factors. On the other hand, the athlete may be concentrating on a cue thought, a feeling inside, a strategy, a past performance, or a future performance, all internal thoughts. One can concentrate on external or internal factors and can also focus attention on a single object or several things at once (Nideffer, 1981). If one does not thoroughly understand this concept, it is easy to miscommunicate about concentration. This chapter will focus on two very important techniques to improve concentration: mental routines and mental rehearsal. These two techniques employ all phases of concentration and mastery of them predisposes the athlete to succeed.

# Mental Routines

Concentration during competition is critical. The athlete must be able to attend to various internal and external cues. Pressure, unforeseen occurrences, and injury can break an athlete's concentration. Mental and physical routines can help an athlete maintain his or her concentration.

Utilizing physical and mental routines, or systematic rituals set the athlete up for success. The athlete is focused and able to control distractions if these routines are adhered to. There will be less chance for self-doubting or stress-producing thoughts, and there will be less chance for a wandering mind. A routine is built upon appropriate physical and mental sequencing.

Some athletes equate routines and superstitions. However, superstitions begin when an athlete inadvertently associates a positive experience in sport with an unrelated source. Superstitions can enhance confidence, but generally they will not hold up over time, because they are based on irrational associations. Physical and mental routines are what help to build lasting *confidence* and *consistent* performances.

Physical routines have been employed for years in all facets of sports. They vary greatly among athletes, but in general they set up the biomechanics for the operative athletic skill. Physical routines, without their mental counterparts, however, can become little more than superstition. We must mentally prepare the athlete as well. The physical routine may be consistent, though the athlete's mind is wandering. Typically this is known as "going through the motions." The key to successful concentration, therefore, is to combine physical and mental routines.

Every athlete has the ability to concentrate. In fact, for all practical purposes, each athlete has the same concentration potential. Even the poorest athletes may have great powers of concentration. However, his or her concentration may be misdirected. The vividness and clarity of the athlete's concentration is impressive, but it is focused on the wrong subject. In other words, the athlete is concentrating vividly, but on exactly the wrong thing. The *ability* to concentrate, therefore, is not the key. The focus of concentration is the foundation of consistent and confident performance. Developing a mental routine then, is taking the innate ability to concentrate and consciously directing the focus in the right direction.

There are four phases or steps to mental routines which, when combined, give meaning to the word "concentration." Each phase is equally important to a successful performance. Phase one is "observation." In this phase, the athlete takes notice of the surroundings and *observes the external information associated with the field of play*, absorbing all that is pertinent. The second phase is "strategy." Here the athlete digests the external information and adopts *a plan or a course of action*. For example, adjustments for wind or a slippery surface may be in order. The third phase is "visualization." In this phase the *performance is visualized ahead of time*. The athlete fixes his or her eyes on the field of play—crossbar, lane, goal, rim, etc . . . and envisions the event in a positive, yet realistic manner. The fourth phase is the "belief cue." Here the athlete activates *a cue word or phrase* which will elicit the proper technique and mental set. The athlete's mind is fixed on this belief cue, which allows the body to *flow* without mental interference. A powerful belief cue for most athletes is the word "trust."

Each step of the routine readies the athlete to react with trust and minimizes extraneous mental interference. *It is mental interference which diverts the message sent from the brain to the muscles.* The four-step routine promotes systematic and thorough concentration. See Figure 6.1, "Cook's Model of Concentration."

Effective concentration involves the ability to shift from phase to phase, prior to and during performance. It involves making the transi-

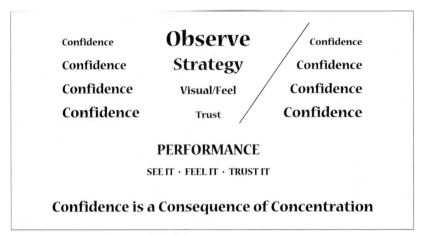

Figure 6.1   Cook's Model of Concentration

tion from phase to phase and avoiding overemphasizing any one step. By consciously going through these steps before each performance, the athlete is systematically programming his or her mind for success. The process of concentration becomes habitual and the mind has no time to wander or to become distracted.. The athlete is establishing a disciplined thought process which will help establish confidence regarding the outcome of the event. This four step mental routine—*observation, strategy, visualization, and belief cue*—will assist the athlete in his or her search for effective concentration. Examples of the four-step routine are given for different sports in Table 6-1.

## Mental Rehearsal

Concentration for hours and even days before an event is as important to success as concentration during the event. Pre-event concentration is usually described in terms such as imagery, mental practice, mental rehearsal, or visualization. It has been said, "We cannot become what we cannot see ourselves becoming." If this is true, then the way an athlete thinks about an upcoming event can be vitally important to his or her success. Therefore, it is important for the athlete to concentrate

## Table 6.1    Mental Routines for Sport Performance

### Golf

1. **Observe**:   Picture the golf hole, see the hazards, distance to the hole, direction of wind, lie of the ball.
2. **Strategy**:   Choose target, type of shot to be made, club selection.
3. **Visualize**:   Visualize the shot; feel the shot.
4. **Cue**:   "Trust" or "Tempo"

### Free Throw

1. **Observe**:   Look at the entire court, check time, score.
2. **Strategy**:   Relax; one fluid, continuous movement.
3. **Visualize**:   Visualize the shot (spin of ball, trajectory, swish ).
4. **Cue**:   Trust."

### Baseball/Softball (Batter)

1. **Observe**:   Where are the fielders, base-runners, any signals from the coaches
2. **Strategy**:   Where is the ball to be hit, what pitch to anticipate.
3. **Visualize**:   Visualize the direction of the hit; feel the hit.
4. **Cue**:   'Drive the ball."

### Baseball/Softball(Pitcher)

1. **Observe**:   Focus on entire field, position of players, the count.
2. **Strategy**:   What pitch to throw; batter's tendencies.
3. **Visualize**:   Picture the pitch, see the movements of the pitch.
4. **Cue**:   "Trust."

### Tennis/Volleyball

1. **Observe**:   See the court, position of opponent, sun, shading, crowd, score.
2. **Strategy**:   Offensive strategy, i.e., placement of serve or shot; defensive strategy for the return (i.e., attack the net).
3. **Visualize**:   Visualize the serve, feel the serve.
4. **Cue**:   'Extension."

### Track (Pole Vault)

1. **Observe**:   See the stadium, check the wind, surface, what events are taking place that might be distracting.
2. **Strategy**:   Adjustments needed for height, wind, etc.
3. **Visualize**:   Visualize the jump.
4. **Cue**:   "Pace."

on positive and constructive images before the competition. Techniques for pre-event concentration can be taught.

Mental rehearsal (pre-event, internal concentration) is the creation of an event in the mind. Mentally rehearsing is making a concerted effort to establish a positive, yet realistic picture of an upcoming performance, employing thoughts, feelings, and actions. This sort of concentration must be taught and nurtured—it does not just happen. In fact for most of us, images of failure tend to occupy our minds because of the fear of failure.

Positive mental rehearsal allows the athlete to deal with an upcoming event and the challenges associated with it in advance. This increases the athlete's confidence level because it promotes a feeling of being prepared, of being in control. Mental rehearsal techniques also help athletes to learn new skills more quickly and thoroughly.

Mental rehearsal works because the body reacts to what it perceives. The physiological system cannot differentiate between real and imagined stimuli. For instance, after being awakened by a nightmare the body perspires and the heart rate increases. In other words, we react to unconscious thoughts. Mental rehearsal allows the athlete to simulate a positive performance over and over so that the body is conditioned to react to the "real" event as it would to the "imagined" event. Theoretically, the body will perform successfully in competition as it did in the athlete's rehearsal.

Two proven types of mental rehearsal strategies can be used by athletes: mastery rehearsal, and mental toughness rehearsal. Though both involve mentally rehearsing an upcoming event, they are distinctly different in their purpose.

## Mastery Rehearsal

Quite simply, mastery rehearsal occurs when the athlete mentally practices *mastering* an event. The athlete mentally rehearses the performance in a very positive, yet realistic manner. The perfect performance is created in the mind and mentally experienced over and over again. This rehearsal includes skills, movements, strategies, environment, sensual or physical feelings, and emotions.

To develop the skill of mastery rehearsal, the athlete must first write a script of the perfect performance that he or she hopes to achieve. The script should include activities which take place throughout the day of the event—waking-up, eating breakfast, driving to the competition, warming-up, competing, and the immediate post-competitive experience. Each of the senses should be incorporated as the athlete attempts to pre-create the sights, sounds, smells, etc. of the event. The script should utilize positive affirmations and be written in the first person, present positive tense, such as: "I am relaxed and ready to compete," or "I feel energized and confident as the game begins." The script should be specific yet brief, so that when it is read it will be between three to five minutes in length. Keeping the script brief is important since it will allow the athlete to utilize it often, even in the midst of a busy daily schedule.

Once the script has been written, the coach can help by reviewing it and adding positive suggestions when necessary. The athlete then records the script on an audio-cassette tape. An example of a creative concentration script appears in Appendix B.

Taping the script allows the athlete to literally hear positive self-talk. To help create the appropriate mood and emotional level, the athlete can add music according to his or her own taste. Having the script and music reflect the athlete's personality enhances his or her receptivity to the tape. This increases the likelihood that the athlete will derive maximum benefit from this technique.

The athlete now has a mental rehearsal tool which is very personal, in that it is a pre-creation of the event through the athlete's eyes and is drawn from personal experience. It is the athlete's own voice and music selection, and it is an expression of confidence and belief which the athlete has personally created. Because this tape has been recorded in his or her own words, the language should reflect the speech patterns and grammar unique to each athlete. The mastery tape can now become a powerful asset as the athlete trains and prepares for an upcoming athletic contest.

The tape can be effectively used during the week or two prior to competition. The athlete should listen to the tape three to four times a day if possible. The key is for the athlete to *experience* the tape and not merely listen to it. Effective times for experiencing the tape are prior to going to sleep each night, immediately after waking-up in the morning, between classes, and just prior to a workout or competition. With a walkman cassette player the athlete can use the tape conveniently and privately in almost any setting.

## Mastery Rehearsal Techniques

- Imagine mastering the sport performance—*mastery*.

- Write a script describing the total experience—pre-event, event, post-event.

- Use first person affirmations—"I" statements.

- Include descriptions of
    1. Environmental considerations.
    2. Senses—sights, sounds, smells, etc.
    3. Movements and feelings associated with the entire event.

- Record on a cassette tape.

- Use music or sound effect.

- Limit tape to three to five minutes.

- Listen to it several times a day.

# Mental Toughness Rehearsal

The athlete now has used mastery rehearsal to prepare for and practice the perfect performance. The athlete has mentally rehearsed mastering the event. Realistically, however, in any competition many variables affect the outcome. An athlete who enters competition completely confident must anticipate potential distractions, and know exactly how to respond to them. How effectively the athlete responds to obstacles will be a significant factor in determining competitive success. Mental toughness rehearsal teaches the athlete to respond effectively to the unpredictability of competitive situations.

Typically, athletes encounter obstacles that they can control as well as those that are beyond their control. One can control obstacles that that can be anticipated, prepared for, and prevented. As for obstacles that cannot be controlled, the athlete can learn to control his or her reactions, thoughts, and emotions with the obstacles.

Just as the athlete uses mastery rehearsal to prepare for the perfect performance, he or she can also use mental toughness rehearsal to effectively cope with obstacles which may be encountered in competition. Mental toughness rehearsal is used before competition to prepare for things that could possibly go wrong. This technique assists the athlete in overcoming self-doubt. Instead of entering an event worrying "what if . . ." the athlete confidently approaches the event knowing "if this happens, . . . I will aggressively and effectively respond in this manner." Obstacles can include a broken shoelace, bad lane assignment, inclement weather, an argument with a boyfriend or girlfriend, tough competition, late change in entry, and the opponents' unpredictable strategy. When an obstacle is perceived as threatening, the athlete frequently reacts with irrational, confused, even panicked thoughts. In essence, he or she loses control. Effective coping, however, involves rationally assessing the situation and identifying and exercising appropriate and effective responses.

The first step in mental toughness rehearsal is for the athlete to anticipate the distractions and obstacles which may be faced in competition. A good method for doing this is to write a list, on the left side of a sheet of paper, identify situations which have been obstacles or caused distractions in the past. The list can include situations that were under the athlete's control and those that were not. Next, add to this list similar situations which are likely to be faced in the future.

The athlete must be honest and specific. He or she may perceive that this is a list of excuses for failing. Mental toughness rehearsal is designed to turn excuses into opportunities and challenges. Though the list on the left side of the page acknowledges negative things, it is a necessary process for the next step.

This step requires the athlete to develop positive, self-enhancing, and rational responses or solutions to each obstacle listed. These responses should be written on the right side of the page, opposite the corresponding obstacle. Each response should include the athlete's thought process relative to the problem. The initial stage in changing behavior is to attack the problem in this sort of non-emotional rational setting. Once the responses have been carefully thought out and written down, the athlete will be able to call upon them in the "heat of battle." The athlete will realize that these responses are much more likely to lead to success than typical self-defeating responses. This is the origin of mental toughness.

The remaining steps in the mental toughness rehearsal techniques are very similar to those which make up mastery rehearsal. The athlete should now write a script for the upcoming performance, incorporating the list of potential obstacles and the corresponding positive responses. Again, the athlete should use "I" affirmations, such as "I will overcome by . . . " or "I will respond by . . . " As in mastery rehearsal, skills, movements, strategies, environment, sensual or physical feelings, and emotions should be incorporated so that the athlete verbalizes all aspects of the challenge. In the script, the athlete may respond to negative emotions, such as anger, frustration, and helplessness, feelings which invariably arise when we face obstacles which negatively affect performance.

Practicing such techniques can make an athlete believe that he or she is mentally tough. Such a belief breeds confidence and an aggressive orientation toward overcoming obstacles instead of fearing that something might go wrong. Anticipating the obstacle and preparing the response ahead of time sets the athlete up for success.

> **Anticipation and preparation is the key to mental toughness.**

The script can then be taped onto a cassette using music or sound effects as desired. It should last from three to five minutes, being brief enough to be used often. The mental toughness tape is to be listened to along with the mastery tape a week before the competition. The last few days before competition, the athlete should focus only on mastery rehearsal and eliminate the mental toughness tape. This will allow the athlete's mind to focus on a mastery performance. It is important to go into the competition believing that such a performance will take place though preparation for unforeseen challenges is the underpinning of this approach. The athlete does not want to enter the competition expecting things to go wrong or looking for problems. The beauty of the mental toughness tape is that responses to potential problems have been thought through and can be called up when appropriate. The mental toughness tape becomes another powerful tool to be used to foster creative concentration by way of imaging techniques, the ultimate goal being improved performances.

## Mental Toughness Rehearsal Techniques

- Imagine an upcoming competition with potential obstacles and distractions—anticipation.

- Develop responses or solutions that are positive, self-enhancing, and rational—preparation.

- Write a script describing the total experience—pre-event, event, post-event components.

- Use first person affirmations—"I" statements.

- Include descriptions of:

     1. Environmental considerations

     2. Senses—sights, sounds, smells, etc.

     3. Movements and feelings associated with the entire event.

- Record on a cassette tape.

- Use music or sound effects.

- Limit tape to three to five minutes.

- Listen to it once a day, up to three or four days before competition.

The combined use of mental and physical routines, the mastery rehearsal tape, and the mental toughness rehearsal tape gives the athlete a comprehensive means to creative concentration. Exercising these various techniques, the athlete can expect a masterful performance, be prepared to cope with any obstacle, and know how to effectively concentrate during the performance.

## References

Nideffer, R. M. (1981). *The ethics and practice of applied sport psychology.* Ithaca, N.Y.: Mouvement Publications.

Rotella, R. J. (1981). Learned effectiveness: A model for maximizing human potential. Bunker, L.K. and Rotella, R. J. (Eds.), *Sport psychology: Psychological considerations in maximizing sport performance.* University of Virginia, HPER Dept Press.

# Composure

Emotional control and stability are psychological traits common to successful coaches and athletes in all sports. The ability to manage one's emotional responses to stressful competitive situations is rudimentary to maximizing athletic performance.

The emotionality of coaches and athletes is affected by the interrelationship of stress, anxiety, and arousal or activation. It is necessary to understand and properly manage these factors in order to have a healthy and productive approach to the athletic environment.

Coaches and athletes have been victims of emotional mismanagement in a variety of ways. We are all familiar with the behavioral signs of such mismanagement: performance fluctuations, physical and mental staleness, burnout, medical problems (e.g., ulcers, nervousness, headaches, insomnia, high blood pressure), traumatization or "choking", and poorly executed motor skills.

It is important for coaches and athletes to realize that such disruptive responses in competitive athletics can be managed once they are recognized and understood. To promote such an understanding this chapter will present an educational overview of the emotional factors that affect athletic performance. We will also introduce a variety of management strategies which can be utilized by coaches and athletes to control such factors and enhance performance.

## Stress And The Athletic Environment

Participation in the world of athletics is very attractive due to the challenges, rewards, and enjoyment inherent in such an environment. Although one's first ventures into athletics are often recreational in nature, they frequently evolve into more sophisticated and demanding endeavors as talents are tested in competitive arenas.

Such an evolution is very attractive to persons who researchers have described as "stress seekers." (Cratty, 1989) Many coaches and athletes derive great satisfaction from their struggles to overcome the obstacles presented by sport. Yet such struggles can create emotional conflict for many sport participants. This dilemma is well expressed by the axiom, "the more an endeavor excites you, the more it exhausts you."

In order to perform effectively as coaches and athletes, physiological and psychological mechanisms should be employed that will help participants achieve a balance in a world that emphasizes achievement and success via athletic performance. The ability of athletes and coaches to adapt to the physical and emotional stress of athletic competition can become their greatest asset as they strive to create a healthy, productive, and stimulating atmosphere in which their talents can be developed and realized.

## Stress And The Training Of Athletes

Athletes and coaches are aware of the importance of conditioning programs that will enable them to adapt to the physical and psychological stresses inherent in sport participation. Such conditioning programs seek to eliminate or reduce stress reactions resulting from physical, social, or psychological events. Anticipation and imagination are examples of such stress reactions. (Girdano & Everly, 1986)

The athlete learns to adapt to the stress of competition and training by being introduced to progressively demanding workloads designed to improve conditioning and fitness. Training and competitive schedules are appropriately designed to provide physical and mental challenges which are commensurate with the athlete's experience, fitness, and skill levels. In essence, prudent application of stress and stressors is essential for the athlete's development.

However, overstressing the athlete through inappropriate training and competitive scheduling can lead to a poor performance. The coach's role is to condition the athlete by selecting appropriate training workloads which gradually prepare the athlete for the rigors of competition.

A sound training program will stimulate a good performance rather than exhaust the athlete. The fitness that results from sound training will prepare the athlete for the rigors and stress of competition. It will also help to make an athlete mentally tough, confident, and persistent. All of these attributes contribute to successful performance. But there is no substitute for adequate physical preparation for competition. It is the first and most important step toward achieving successful athletic performances.

## Anxiety

The most common emotion that disrupts performance in competitive athletics is anxiety. It is an abnormal apprehension regarding the impact of present and future events upon performance. Anxiety may also manifest itself as fear concerning the outcome of athletic events. An anxious athlete may perceive competition as threatening (Cratty, 1989).

The athlete and coach are attracted to the excitement their sport provides in terms of facing the unknown. This unpredictability can also cause apprehension and discomfort. Extremely anxious athletes experience an uneasiness which interferes with their concentration and results in a poor or subpar performance. Many anxious athletes find this state so psychologically uncomfortable they eventually leave the highly competitive athletic environment.

One of the most disturbing manifestations of anxiety in athletes is traumatization or "choking" under the stress of competition. Immobilized by fear, the anxious athlete is tense, nervous, and unable to perform well. This results in frustration and disappointment for themselves and their coach.

On the other hand, coaches' anxiety is manifested by an inability to make decisions. The decision-making powers of coaches and athletes are diminished by "information overload." This phenomenon is best expressed by the quote, "Indecision is the sign of a fearful mind."

Besides "choking" and indecision, another disruptive behavioral pattern of the anxious athlete or coach is their inability to recognize and/or pay attention to their performance cues during competition. Since athletes have an understandable tendency to focus solely on outcome goals (e.g., times, points scored, batting average), they often forget their performance goals. Performance goals refer to the execution of skills and techniques which contribute to the attainment of outcome goals. For example, a pole vaulter may want to win a competition, to make All-American or to make an international team (outcome goal), but he must first accomplish his performance goals (e.g., approach, including check marks, pole plant, proper alignment at take-off, penetration after take-off). In essence the athlete must be calm enough immediately prior to and during competition to effectively bring to bear all of his or her skills.

Another concern regarding the performance of the anxious athlete has to do with the relationship between anxiety and muscular tension. This phenomena is called "tension tie-up." It is experienced by every athlete at one time or another and is characterized by an inability to perform skills in a relaxed manner. In short, "tension tie-up" restricts an athlete's fluidity. This condition occurs in athletes who are "overpowering" their skills, or simply trying too hard to consciously effect the outcome of their event rather than relaxing and allowing their training and experience to work for them in a very natural way.

Although there are a variety of fears which tend to affect the performance of the anxious athlete (e.g., fear of pain and injury, fear of aggression, fear of rejection by the coach, fear of success), fears associated with losing and winning tend to have the greatest impact upon their performance. (Cratty, 1983)

Some athletes may tend to avoid success because of the leadership responsibilities that tend to follow it, particularly because of expectations of continued success in their sport. It is, very simply, less demanding and stressful to be average. Bruce Ogilvie (1968), an American pioneer in the field of sport psychology, coined the phrase "success phobia" and pointed out that the stress of high-level competition frequently produce feelings of social isolation and unhealthy assertiveness or the desire to "beat others." These feeling, together with the pressure to continue to win once the athlete has reached the top, combine to produce rebellion against winning. (Cratty, 1989)

Thus, fears regarding losing stem from guilt feelings at not performing as well as one could and from the fear of disappointing coaches, family, and friends as a result of poor performances.

It is important that coaches recognize the influence they have upon the emotional states of their athletes. Since the coach has no direct control over the outcome of an athletic event, it is very easy for them to project feelings of anxiety to their athletes. The coach must strive to be a model of emotional stability for the athlete, developing the security and confidence he or she needs to perform in a relaxed manner under stressful competitive situations.

**Identification of the Anxious Athlete.** Observation of the athlete's behavior and performance before, during, and after competitive events is one of the most effective ways to identify the athlete who tends to be inappropriately anxious. Observation can be employed by the coach and/or sport psychologist or, by the athlete. The coach and athlete must first recognize the behavioral signs and symptoms of the highly anxious athlete. Once the anxious athlete is identified, steps can be taken to aid the athlete in adapting to the competitive stresses which may be adversely affecting their performance and their physical and psychological well being.

Behavioral symptoms of the highly anxious athlete include: preoccupation and overemphasis on outcome goals (winning), excessive nervousness, tendencies to over- or under-train; inadequate or excessive warm-up, boastfulness, frequent injury, irritability, muscle tension, poor execution of skills, insomnia, loss of appetite, and performance fluctuations.

Physiological symptoms and responses related to the stress of athletic competition include: increased heart rate, heightened blood pressure and respiration rates, nausea, headaches, ulcers, labored or shallow breathing, gastrointestinal disturbances, profuse sweating, excessive fatigue, and muscle soreness. In more extreme cases of anxiety, athletes may display signs of personality disintegration including weeping, anger, self-imposed isolation, and the use of alcohol and drugs (Cratty, 1983).

Sport psychologists have also utilized more sensitive techniques to identify the anxious athlete as well as further define the types of anxiety experienced by individuals. Sport psychologists have employed psychometric evaluations (paper and pencil inventories/questionnaires) to study anxiety. The *Sport Competition Anxiety Test* (SCAT) developed by Rainier Martens (1977) has been utilized to assess individual differences in the perception of competitive situations. (Sonstroem, 1984) This evaluative tool, if properly administered and interpreted, can be extremely useful in identifying an athlete whose performance may be hindered by competitive stress.

# Arousal

Although the concept of arousal has been closely associated with the emotional state of anxiety, in the sport context it refers to the degree of activation within the body. Activation can range from deep sleep to extreme excitement. For our purposes, arousal refers to the athlete's *level of excitement*.

It is important for the coach and athlete to understand the inter-relation of anxiety and arousal. The highly anxious and over-aroused athlete is most susceptible to fluctuations and breakdowns in his or her performances. In general, the successful athlete is prepared, self-confident, relaxed, and only *moderately* aroused (Bunker, 1985).

In their efforts to motivate athletes, coaches sometimes have the tendency to "overpsych" or "overactivate" their charges. The key to achieving maximum performance is identification of the appropriate arousal levels for each athlete based upon the motor skill complexities of the event. Once this is accomplished the athlete will be "psyched up, not out." (Bunker, 1985)

Depending on the motor skill complexity of a particular athletic activity, an athlete should be aroused to a level above his or her normal resting, but not to the level of over-arousal. Athletes who are apathetic or under-aroused may require experiences that cause an increase in their arousal levels, while athletes whose arousal levels are already quite high prior to competition may profit from reducing their arousal level. (Bunker, 1985)

Coaches should be aware that increased drive or arousal will facilitate the performance of well-learned skills, whereas similar levels of heightened arousal will hamper the learning or acquisition of poorly-learned skills or strategies. In essence, new skills should be well-learned (drilled) before they are executed in the competitive setting. Similarly, new skills should be introduced to athletes well in advance of competition in order to keep arousal levels low. It also helps athletes in the initial stages of learning their skills to practice in isolation with only the coach present to provide feedback and monitor their training. Practice in the presence of teammates tends to distract the athlete, to increase their arousal, and disrupts skill acquisition and performance. When introducing new skills to athletes the coach should keep arousal levels low by providing interesting, well organized, and enjoyable practice sessions.

Great caution should be exercised in the use of competition to motivate athletes. Placing athletes in competitive situations will disrupt and retard the learning and the performance of recently acquired skills. Conscientious practice, punctuated by the use of drills directed towards "overlearning" skills, will yield the best competitive results.

Additionally, the coach should focus on the relationship between arousal or activation levels and the task demands of athletic skills. Task demands can be defined in terms of complexity, physical requirements (speed, strength, endurance), environmental conditions, psychological and emotional factors.

In general, a high level of arousal is essential for optimal performance in gross motor activities (e.g., jumping, throwing, running) involving strength, endurance, and speed. A high level of arousal (motivation/activation) will, however, disrupt performances involving complex motor skill patterns (e.g., pitching a baseball, hammer throw, foul shooting, etc.), fine muscle movement, coordination, steadiness, and concentration.

Various sport skills require different levels of arousal for optimal performance. As the athlete's arousal level moves from drowsiness to being alert, performance improves, but movement from alertness to high excitement leads to the deterioration of performance. Therefore, a mid-range (general alertness) or moderate levels of arousal will promote the best performance.

Evaluation of the following factors by coach and athlete prior to competition is essential for determining the appropriate arousal levels:

- the athlete's personality and predisposition to emotional performance interruption;

- the athlete's skill level and abilities;

- the type of athletic skill or task the athlete will attempt to execute and/or implement;

- the environmental conditions;

- the athlete's feeling of competency in relation to the athletic skill or task;

- and the effect of social influences on the athlete's arousal level. (Bunker, 1985, p. 159)

# Control and Regulation of Anxiety and Arousal Levels for Maximum Performance

As previously stated, the management of stress-related emotional responses (anxiety and physical arousal/activation) is an essential part of effective athletic performance. A variety of psycho-physical strategies that promote stress management have been developed and effectively utilized by sport psychologists, coaches, and athletes. These strategies include: relaxation training, autogenics, biofeedback, mental imagery or visualization, and model training.

Initially, the athlete should be made aware that competition can enhance their performance because it demands the efficient execution of skills they have so diligently practiced and developed. The athlete should look forward to competition as an opportunity to improve and realize athletic talents.

Competitions can help to ready the athlete emotionally and physically for effective performances. Most importantly, athletes need to realize that their nervousness regarding the outcome of an athletic contest is natural, and if controlled, will help them perform optimally.

Once aware of the adverse effect that the mismanagement of emotional responses can have upon performance, athletes can utilize relaxation, autogenic, biofeedback, and arousal control training to avoid "tension tie-up" and enhance their performance.

## Relaxation Training

Relaxation has been described as a physical or mental condition which enables one to accomplish more than is possible at the conscious level. (Bennett & Pravitz, 1982)

Physical relaxation, the opposite of "tension tie-up", is characterized by a loosening of the muscles. Of equal concern to coaches and
athletes is mental relaxation or relaxation of the conscious or thinking mind. When relaxed, our conscious or thinking mind slows down,
is "stilled," or "calmed." (Bennett & Pravitz, 1982) Excessive muscular tension is detrimental to skillful, coordinated performances and can
be triggered by mental input which generates worry, apprehension, or
fear. Moreover, inappropriate thoughts and feelings can deter an athlete's performance. Relaxation techniques can rid the muscles of tension that interferes with performance and help the athlete to lessen or
eliminate the effects of undesirable thoughts and feelings (Harris,
1986).

More specifically, relaxation training can be helpful in removing
localized tension (e.g., headaches, low back pain), in recovering from
fatigue or injuries, in promoting sleep and reducing insomnia, and in
enhancing muscular coordination thus promoting skillful performance
(Harris, 1986).

Progressive relaxation training as developed by Jacobson (1938),
creates a state of muscular awareness through conscious control of
peripheral skeletal muscles, thus bringing emotional states under better self control. Jacobson's methods have been used by the medical community to treat people suffering from hypertension and various emotional disturbances. Essentially, the technique involves placing
individuals in a comfortable position and then helping them to gain
an awareness of the muscular tension in their bodies or in various body
parts (Cratty, 1983).

Progressive relaxation exercises involve contracting a specific muscle group, holding the contraction for several seconds, then relaxing.
The letting go, or relaxation phase, makes one aware what absence of
tension feels like. One learns that relaxation can be voluntarily induced
by consciously releasing tension in a muscle (Harris, 1986). A sample
of a progressive relaxation training program can be found in Appendix A.

## Autogenic training

Autogenic (self-generating) training concentrates on the autonomic muscular reactions as well as the athlete's mental state. In this technique, individuals are asked to relax and to imagine various body parts growing warmer. They are helped to regulate autonomic responses and body processes (e.g., heart rates, respiration rates), and are asked to imagine various body parts "becoming heavier." This technique can also be employed in the regulation of mental states, arousal control, and visualization. (Cratty, 1983)

Additional forms of autogenic training which can help athletes control and regulate their emotional states and activation levels are self-hypnosis, meditation, "thought stopping" or "self-talk" techniques, and visualization or mental imagery. These techniques create a climate conducive to effective subconscious programming, and promote creative thinking, problem solving, and mental rehearsal of goal attainment strategies. Desired outcomes of such training are improved self-confidence, consistency, concentration, and motor skill execution (Bennett & Pravitz, 1982).

Naturally, we hope that athletes willingly engage in positive self-talk to mentally affirm their abilities and skills prior to performance. In reality, however, this is very often not the case. If we believe that *thought precedes action* then we must do all that we can to promote positive thoughts regarding their abilities, skills, and the outcome of their performances.

Athletes can learn to control their thoughts through the following three-step mental process:

1. *Recognize negative thinking and decode to think positively.* Athletes need to be aware that they are thinking negatively and that they can choose not to think this way. Negative thoughts are a natural part of athletic performance but the athlete can dispel such thoughts and refocus his or her thoughts on a successful performance.

Negative thoughts can soon escalate into attitudes which pre-dispose an athlete to failure. Common negative self-talk such as, "I hope I do well," leads to doubt and worry. Likewise, negative self-talk such as, "I have to do well," can lead to stress and anxiety.

Positive self-talk, such as, "I can do well," reflect and reaffirm an athlete's confidence in his or her skills and abilities.

2. *Physically interrupt negative thoughts.* Athletes can interrupt and stop negative thoughts by clapping their hands once sharply, snapping their fingers, or firmly squeezing the forefinger and thumb together. Other physical behaviors can be employed by the athlete and should be used as soon as he or she becomes aware of counter-productive thinking.

3. *Replace negative thoughts with positive thoughts.* The final step of this process requires the athlete to positively refocus his or her thoughts on the task at hand. "I am relaxed, energized, and ready to perform well today," is an example of a positive replacement statement for thoughts of worry, doubt, and anxiety.

Autogenic training is one of the most practical and effective mental training techniques available to athletes. Essentially, the various types of autogenic training involve the following sequential steps:

- *Relaxation Phase*—The athlete utilizes a particular relaxation technique which induces physical and mental calmness. The athlete's initial goal during this phase is to be free of muscular tensions. Once accomplished, he or she seeks to attain an "alpha" state between sleep and full consciousness. This is the state we achieve just prior to sleep when we are somewhat drowsy and totally relaxed.

- *Programming Phase*—Once physical and mental relaxation are achieved, the athlete is ready to present suggestions to his or her subconscious mind. These suggestions take the form of mental pictures and images of successful outcomes of their training and performance experiences. This visualization process can be composed of mental images which recall the athlete's most enjoyable and successful athletic experiences or images of desired future successes. The athlete's initial goal in the programming phase is to

*Picture themselves experiencing and enjoying athletic success.*

The next goal of the programming phase is to itemize the steps which must be taken to achieve this success. In this phase the athlete is encouraged to focus on specific strategies and skills that will promote a successful performance. The athlete mentally rehearses his or her skills and actually pictures him or herself performing these skills successfully in training and competition. A mental plan is established which specifically and vividly describes what steps an athlete needs to take to achieve success.

- *Associative Phase*—In order to help an athlete recall the previously programmed suggestions, athletes should establish cues (colors, words, numbers, etc.) which will trigger an appropriate response. In competition, for example, an athlete might have a number cue that triggers the appropriate arousal level. Or, an athlete may relax and be reminded of skills by focusing on uniform color, or by repeating a word or phrase, such as "relax," or by an affirmation, such as "I am performing well." These cues will help the athlete to perform well and to make the best use of his or her training and talents.

- *Mind to Muscle Phase*—In order to be effective, autogenic training must be practiced on a daily basis. At least one 20–30 minute session should be conducted just prior to training or competition. It should take place in an environment that is quiet, free of distractions, and conducive to relaxation and concentration.

## Biofeedback

Athletes can learn to gauge their ability to relax by utilizing biofeedback techniques. Such techniques teach the athletes to "listen" to their bodies by becoming aware of body signals that indicate inappropriate physiological or muscular response. Physiological instrumentation can make the athlete aware of heart rate changes, respiratory fluctuations, brain wave patterns, and muscle tension. Such responses may be potentially detrimental to performance if not regulated and controlled. Cratty (1989) claims that biofeedback provides:

1. ...the athlete with objective evidence of emotional arousal states which have been experienced subjectively in the past;

2. ...a direction (visual or auditory feedback) toward which the athlete may focus attention and thus anxiety, rather than internalizing such fears;

3. ...objective criteria against which the athlete may compare transitory feelings of anxiety and objective ways he or she can contrast momentary internalized mood states with objective information obtained through the apparatus used;

4. ...permit the athlete and clinician to objectively work out ways to adjust anxiety levels to those that appear amenable to optimum performance (p. 132).

## Arousal Control Training

An autogenic training method which incorporates biofeedback into an effective emotion management program is arousal control training (Vernacchia, Austin, VandenHazel, & Roe, 1992). Essentially the athlete is taught to regulate his or her own arousal level in light of past, present, and future performances. This method of arousal control associates arousal level with numbers ranging from 1–10 (e.g., 1 = the lowest level of arousal and 10 = the highest arousal level). Athletes are asked to recall and visualize their peak athletic performance and associate this feeling with a number from 1–10 which approximates their arousal or excitement level at the time of this performance. The idea is that an athlete who is readying himself or herself for competition can replicate the physical and emotional arousal state achieved prior to a best performance. Using a number to represent arousal level helps the athlete to remember an ideal arousal state.

Athletes' ability to regulate their arousal levels during performances has been reported. For example, a long jumper may use the number 7 to represent his or her arousal level while at the head of the runway just prior to jumping. This number will increase (i. e., 7–8–9) during the approach phase of the jump until it reaches 10 at the take-off board. (Vernacchia, et. al., 1992) Obviously this is a refined application of arousal control training but with the appropriate amount of practice athletes can learn to integrate this emotion management strategy into their performances.

## Practice and Coaching Considerations for Reducing Anxiety

There are a variety of technique and behavioral strategies that coaches and athletes can employ in their daily training routines that will help prepare them for competition.

Coaches must be constantly aware of the effect their attitudes and behavior have upon their athletes. It is important for the coach to stress a process approach to sport participation and athletic performance. Athletes should be encouraged to enjoy the pleasurable aspects of the athletic experience (e.g., making friends, promoting good health behaviors, self-improvement, attaining goals). Many coaches and athletes lose sight of the most pleasurable aspects of sport because they are preoccupied with the mechanics of training and competition.

Coaches should be cautious about and avoid projecting their anxieties and fears to their athletes. They should present a relaxed and calm demeanor which reflects confidence and control, especially when stressful situations arise. Athletes will feel comfortable, secure, relaxed, and less confused under such leadership.

In many cases, especially with young or inexperienced athletes, the coach may have to relieve or reduce an athlete's stress by accepting responsibility for the results of strategies employed in competition. The coach should discourage the athlete from dwelling on negative performances and make such experiences constructive and educational for the athlete's preparation for future competitions.

Furthermore, coaches should avoid *emotionalization* in preparing their athletes for competition. Pre-competition preparation should be essentially instructive and focus on the successful execution of skills. Athletes should want to win and be successful, but over-emotionalization can diffuse their focus regarding performance cues. For this reason, pre-competitive team meetings should help athletes identify their performance cues and create a belief that if their skills are enthusiastically and accurately executed, successful performances will follow.

Team meetings comprised of "pep-talks" should be replaced by meetings which stress the components of successful athletic performance: offensive and defensive strategies; warm-up procedures; travel plans; training room procedures for treatment and prevention of injuries; and performance cues that elicit the successful execution of sport skills. Athletes should be encouraged to enjoy the competitive atmosphere with statements such as, "These rules are designed to accommodate you and to provide a first-class environment to help you achieve your best performance. Enjoy the competition, the people around you, and give your best effort."

Additional anxiety-reducing strategies which coaches can utilize include: gradually and progressively *desensitizing* the athlete to the various stress related aspects of athletic competition (e.g., have a sprinter run on a relay before competing in open competition); *de-emphasizing* the importance of the athletic contest and the athlete's performance expectations; providing a *diversion* from the approaching competitive situation (e.g., ask athletes to bring homework along while traveling to competitions).

The coach can most effectively prepare athletes for competition by incorporating *model training* into work-out schedules. Model training attempts to simulate in the practice situation the exact conditions the athlete will experience in competition. For example, cross country runners can train at race pace and over terrain that is similar to the course on which they will compete. The coach can also plan for the athletes to race on the course early in the season, or conduct a training session on the race course during the week prior to competition, or arrive one day prior to the competition in order to allow the athletes to familiarize themselves with the race course.

Athletes can also be prepared to perform in stressful performance situations by: *overlearning* their skills or engaging in practice sessions composed of prolonged skill or event drills; establishing a *warm-up routine* which will, in effect, act as a relaxing ritual immediately prior to competitive efforts; engaging in a *light workout* session several hours prior to competing; and by *removing* themselves from the potential over-stimulation of the competitive environment (e.g., stadium or arena) until their event is contested.

The athlete will become more relaxed and able to appropriately control their arousal/activation levels as he or she becomes more experienced. Athletes should be exposed progressively to more difficult competition in light of their developmental characteristics and recent performance results.

# Composure: Principles of Effective Emotion Management

"Playing with emotion" and a passion for athletic excellence will empower and enable athletes to reach their highest levels of personal athletic performance. Coaches are given the task of monitoring and directing the emotions of each athlete who is involved in the competitive athletic arena and can effectively do so by being mindful of the following emotion management principles:

1. *Emotional control and stability are psychological traits common to successful athletes and coaches.* While it is important to play with emotion, coaches and athletes must constantly be aware of how the interrelated components of stress, anxiety, and arousal effect their decision-making ability and motor performance. Poor emotion management can disrupt athletic performance.

2. *Coaches and athletes can learn to adjust and adapt to the stress of the athletic environment.* Coaches and athletes can achieve the emotional balance necessary to thrive and perform effectively in the stressful world of competitive athletics.

3. *Physical stress and emotional stress are interrelated.* This fact is evidenced by the athlete or coach who is overexposed to the rigors of athletic training and/or performance. Care must be taken to commit to a training program and performance schedule which allow individuals to recover from the physical and emotional stress of the athletic environment.

4. *Fear of winning and losing gives rise to anxiety, stress, and ineffective coaching and athletic performance.* Whether real or imagined, an obsessive preoccupation and overemphasis on the positive and negative results of athletic competition can create a fearful mind-set which disrupts effective athletic performance.

5. *Arousal refers to the ability of the athlete to appropriately activate him or herself for athletic competition.* Activation or excitability in competition must correlate to the demands and characteristics of

a performance situation. There is a direct relationship between activation and motor performance, hence the term *excite-ability*.

6. *An athlete's anxiety and arousal levels can be managed and controlled to attain effective performances.* Autogenic training methods such as relaxation, and visualization, and biofeedback can be utilized to manage and control inappropriate physical and emotional responses to the stress of athletic training and competition.

7. *Coaches can create and design a practice and pre-performance environment which will enable athletes to manage their emotions.* Emotion management strategies such as role modeling, avoiding emotionalization, desensitization, model training, and overlearning physical skills through prolonged drill can be integrated into coaching and training methodology in order to help athletes cope with the stresses of athletic competition.

## References

Bennett, J.G., and Pravitz, J.E. (1982). *The miracle of sports psychology.* Englewood Cliffs, New Jersey: Prentice-Hall, Inc.

Bunker, L. (1985). The effect of anxiety and arousal on performance. *Sport psychology: Psychological considerations in maximizing sport performance.* L. Bunker, R. Rotella, and A. Reilly (Eds.). Mouvement Publications.

Cratty, B. J. (1983). *Psychology in contemporary sport,* (2nd Ed.). Englewood Cliffs, New Jersey: Prentice Hall, Inc.

Cratty, B. J. (1989). *Psychology in contemporary sport,* (3rd Ed.). Englewood Cliffs, New Jersey: Prentice Hall, Inc.

Girdano, D.A., and Everly, G.S.(1986) *Controlling stress and tension: A holistic approach,* (2nd). Englewood Cliffs, New Jersey, Prentice-Hall Inc.

Harris, D. V.(1986). Relaxation and energizing techniques for regulation of arousal. *Applied sport psychology: personal growth to peak performance,* J.M. Williams (Ed.) Mountain View, CA: Mayfield Publishing Co.

Jacobson, E.(1938). *Progressive relaxation,* Chicago: The University of Chicago Press.

Martins, R. (1977). *Sport competition anxiety test,* Champaign, IL: Human Kinetics Publisher.

Ogilvie, B. (1968). The unconscious fear of success, " *Quest,* 10, pp. 35-39.

Sonstroem, R. J. (1984). An overview of anxiety in sport. *Psychological foundations of sport,* John Silva, Robert Weinberg (Eds.). Champaign, IL: Human Kinetics Publisher, 1984.

Vernacchia, R. A.; Austin, S.; VandenHazel, M.; and Roe, R. (1992). The influence of self-hypnosis upon the arousal and performance of intercollegiate track and field athletes", *Applied Research in Coaching and Athletics Annual,* 77-91.

# Conducting Effective Practice Sessions

Coaches have long recognized the importance of conducting well organized practice sessions which skillfully prepare their athletes for successful performance in competitive situations. With conscientious practice and a store of successful competitive and training experiences, the athlete can hope to realize his or her athletic potential.

Coaches in all sports realize that they must be excellent teachers to be effective. They must be experts in their sports, understand the learning process, and be able to communicate knowledge to their athletes. As Oxendine (1986) states, *"The teacher-coach must have the ability to detect performance errors, to give the learner clear feedback about those errors, and to provide reinforcement when the slightest improvement is noted."* (p.17)

This chapter presents a variety of practice principles which will promote the acquisition and performance of athletic skills in all sports. Coach and athlete are reminded "practice does not make perfect; perfect, planned, purposeful practice makes perfect." How we practice is as important as what we practice. It also helps establish controllable, predictable, and successful performances.

# Skill Acquisition And The Learning Process

Researchers and learning theorists (Fitts, 1964; Oxendine, 1984; and Robb, 1972) describe three progressive learning stages or phases. Athletes can be said to go through the cognitive, practice, and autonomic stages as they learn the skills that are specific to their sports.

### Cognitive Phase

In this initial stage the athletes attempt to "picture" or visualize the performance of newly introduced skills or techniques. Athletes will often tell their coaches, "I don't see what you mean" after skills are described to them. To help the athletes mentally and physically assimilate new skills, the coach should employ a variety of teaching techniques. The coach may demonstrate how the skill is correctly performed via loop films, videotapes, or demonstrations by highly skilled teammates.

### Practice Phase

This stage, also referred to as the associative or fixation phase of learning, is the stage at which the athlete approaches maximum efficiency through trial and error. At the beginning of this phase, improvement is made rapidly. Progressively less and less change is necessary as performance approaches the optimal level. Feedback from the coach is important during this phase, when athletes are also developing their own ability to monitor themselves and to detect their errors. It is important for the coach to monitor the training sessions closely during this phase, paying particular attention to eliminating factors which can hinder learning (e.g., fatigue, frustration, and boredom). To achieve successful skill performance the coach should encourage attitudes and behaviors which will help the athlete establish consistent training patterns (e.g., self discipline).

## Autonomic Phase

This stage of learning reflects the fruits of conscientious and diligent practice, and is characterized by the relaxed and effective, almost unconscious skill performance. Skills have been practiced so much that they have become habits and once the athlete makes the decision to perform a task, motor responses are automatically triggered (Oxendine, 1986).

## Learning modes

Athletes have three learning modes in which they process information relative to the acquisition of motor skills and tasks: visual, auditory, and feeling (kinesthetic). They are used singularly or in combination to facilitate skill learning.

Many athletes learn best by watching (visual mode) and imitating movement patterns displayed by highly skilled performers. Others assimilate skills better when they are explained and described to them verbally (auditory mode). Some athletes may perform newly acquired skills best after they have physically experienced (body awareness mode) the movement patterns of these skills. The coach must identify the athlete's primary learning mode and provide the appropriate learning instructions. Films, videotapes, and demonstrations will appeal to the visually oriented learner while verbal descriptions and athlete-coach discussions about newly introduced skills will be most productive for athletes who preferred the auditory mode. Similarly, coaches may best instruct some athletes by allowing them the time and opportunity to physically "explore" movement patterns, thereby helping the athlete to develop a "feel" for the newly introduced skill or task.

An interesting method for determining primary learning modes involves observing the athlete's eye movements as skills are being explained to them. Once explanations have been made and while the athlete is absorbing the newly acquired information, he or she may look up (visual learner), to the side (auditory learner), or downward (feeling or kinesthetic learner), thus presenting relevant cues to the coach regarding the athlete's preferred learning mode.

# Reinforcement

Coaches can utilize a variety of incentives when training and preparing their athletes for competitive situations. Learning incentives such as reward or praise, criticism or reproof, knowledge of results (feedback), and social stimulation (cooperation and competition) can be employed either singularly or in combination to elicit the desired behaviors.

### Identifying Educational, Social, and Performance Goals

The specific values, attitudes, and physical skills that the coach wants to develop and assimilate into an athlete's behavioral pattern must first be identified before any reinforcement program is implemented. Such behavioral outcomes can be developed and identified through past experiences and discussion among the coaching staff and selected athletes (e.g., veterans, team captains). Initially educational, social, and performance values and goals will be the focus of such discussions. Eventually, the discussions will identify specific behaviors that will result in the attainment of these values and goals.

An example of possible goal-directed behavioral outcomes for an athletic program would be:

## Educational Goals

- development of "carry-over" attitudes and behaviors that contribute to lifetime health and fitness habits (e.g., nutrition, relaxation techniques, strength development/weight training, aerobic exercise);

- academic achievement;

- development of attitudes which will assist athletes in goal attainment (e.g., commitment, achievement, goal setting techniques);

- development of self-actualizing behaviors including positive self-esteem and self-confidence.

## Social Goals

- establishing friendships;

- relating to individuals of diverse background in order to achieve a common goal;

- developing respect for authority.

## Performance Goals

- acquisition of the physical skills or movement patterns which will enable the athlete to perform effectively in competition;

- organization of practice sessions to aid athletes in acquiring skills;

- utilization of specific training techniques which will promote effective skill learning;

- providing athletes with the psychological skills necessary to facilitate performance in stressful situations (e.g., model training, autogenic training, relaxation training);

- providing appropriate competitive opportunities to stimulate skill development and realize performance goals.

## Positive and Negative Reinforcement

Once the coach identifies the goals of training and competition, he or she must then select appropriate reinforcers that will promote efficient learning and performance of desired behavioral outcomes. To enhance the learning process, coaches employ positive forms of reinforcement to create a productive training and performance environment.

*Positive reinforcement* is preferable to negative reinforcement because it rewards the athlete for performing well. The athlete associates rewards gained with a successful performance and a pleasurable experience results. People generally want to repeat pleasurable experiences and athletes are no different.

*Negative reinforcement* alerts the athlete to errors they have made and reminds the athlete that he or she has yet to perform as desired. Sanctions and criticism can make the athlete fearful and cause him or her to avoid competition. In regards to the use of punishment to motivate athletes, Ronald Smith (1986) states:

> First and foremost is the fact that punishment works by arousing fear. If used excessively, punishment promotes the development of fear of failure, and this is undoubtedly the least desirable form of athletic motivation. If it becomes the predominant motive for athletic performance, it not only decreases enjoyment of the activity but it also increases the likelihood of failure. The athlete who has a strong sense of failure is motivated not by a positive desire to achieve and enjoy the thrill of victory but by a fear of the agony of defeat. Athletic competition is transformed from a challenge into a threat...The research literature also shows that the quickest and most effective way to develop fear of failure is by punishing people when they fail. (pp. 36-37)

Simply put, coaches should reward athletes for good performances and give instructions regarding how they can correct performances. The goal is to make athletes comfortable in the learning environment so that they can improve their skills and perform successfully. This is why coaches are encouraged to reward the "efforts" as well as the "outcomes" when training their athletes.

Coaches should also be aware that learning is accelerated by very frequent positive reinforcement in response to effective performances. The frequency should decrease progressively to accurately gauge learning and retention. Coaches should frequently reinforce the athlete during the "trial and error" stages as new skills are introduced and then reinforce or reward less frequently once skills or behaviors are performed correctly (Oxendine, 1984).

Once skills have been learned (performed correctly on a consistent basis) the coach needs only to reinforce the athlete occasionally. Such partial reinforcement practices will encourage the athlete to persist with their training and with the exercise of learned skills in competitive situations. (Oxendine, 1984)

## Modifying Athletic Behavior

In order to foster and develop maximum achievement in athletic endeavors, the coach should establish reward systems for athletes who perform in a predetermined manner. Such rewards include letter awards, qualifying criteria for local, state, and national competitions, etc. These can serve to keep athletes interested in performing in a purposeful way. Essentially, this type of reinforcement can be viewed as "merit" awards, powerful motivating incentives in any athletic program.

Coaches can direct and successfully modify athletic behavior by employing the following reinforcement principles:

1. *Target Behavioral Objectives.* Identify and establish performance goals and the specific behaviors (skills) with which these goals will be realized.

2. *Stress Positive Reinforcement.* Reward athletes for performing correctly in practice and/or competition. Provide opportunities for athletes to learn or improve skills in a comfortable and encouraging environment.

3. *Provide Feedback When Mistakes Occur.* Emphasize improvement in the learning and performance phases of motor skill acquisition. Mistakes are a natural by-product of the learning and performance process. Provide the athlete with information regarding corrective feedback in order to facilitate learning, minimize mistakes, and develop consistent motor performance patterns.

4. *Reward Athletes Immediately When Skills Are Performed Correctly.* Very simply, reward the athlete when a predetermined behavioral pattern is performed correctly. Reward becomes contingent upon performing correctly.

5. *Link Rewards to Correct Behaviors.* It is also important to make sure athletes know specifically why they received a particular reward. The typical comment, "good job" is inadequate. The athlete must know specifically what he or she did correctly in order to replicate this behavior in future performance situations.

6. *Reward Athletes If They Are Approaching Success.* Many athletic skills are by nature very complex and will be learned over a period of time. To encourage athletes to persist with training and performance tasks, and to prevent frustration, it is helpful to reward athletes if they are "close to" or approximating the exact response you are seeking.

7. *Reward Athletes Occasionally Once They Have Learned A Specific Sport Skill or Movement Pattern.* Help athletes to maintain their interest in practicing and performing their skills by providing partial reinforcement, especially for experienced or veteran performers. Reward athletes every once in awhile after skills are

mastered. This will insure that the athlete will persist at the correct performance of previously learned athletic skills.

# Practice Considerations and the Training of Athletes

There is no secret to achieving success as an athlete. Athletes are successful when they have diligently prepared themselves for competition by engaging in well-organized and scientifically designed practice sessions. Their successes did not stem from chance or luck, unless one gives credence to the definition, "Luck is when preparation meets opportunity." Athletes and coaches often sum up this philosophy in this way: "The more I practice, the luckier I get." More often than not, athletes who compete at highly competitive levels in all sports are dedicated to painstaking preparation. How well we practice will determine how well we perform.

## Conditioning

The initial challenges for the coach and athlete in all training programs have to do with preparing the performer physically and psychologically for the demands and stresses they will be confronted by in practice and competition. Physical conditioning is essential and should precede the more sophisticated aspects of the training program, (e.g., cognitive strategies, peaking, skill acquisition, model training).

Sound conditioning will help the athlete gradually adapt to the stresses of training and competition and should proceed through the initial or "alarm" stage, the resistance stage, and the exhaustion or "overtraining" stage.

- *Initial or "Alarm" Stage.* This is the initial conditioning phase in which the athlete is gradually introduced to the stresses and demands of training. Through gradual exposure to conditioning, the athlete is able to adapt to physiological and psychological stress and soon maintains a "steady state," that is, he or she is capable of meeting the demands of the stressors he or she faces. This is the preconditioning phase which prepares the athlete for more sophisticated training methods. This stage is essential for establishing a conditioning base and usually consists of pre-season or pre-competitive training.

• *Resistance Stage.* Once the athlete has a training foundation, he or she is introduced to more sophisticated conditioning techniques. The athlete will progress to peak conditioning by employing these techniques in intense training bouts. These should be carefully regulated and allow for frequent rest and recovery periods. This is the stage where training makes its impact.

• *Exhaustion or "overtraining" stage.* The athlete should very seldom enter this stage. Once this stage has been entered, the athlete's resistance, developed in stage 2, has been overcome and motor performance deteriorates. Excessive fatigue sets in and the athlete loses their "zip" and competitive zest. If the athlete remains in the exhaustion stage for a prolonged period, the only remedy is REST or a substantial decrease in training workloads and intensities.

These suggestions for phased conditioning are based on the research conducted by exercise physiologists, especially the writing of Hans Selye (1976), whose works emphasize the importance of gradual adaptation to physical and psychological stress. This theory suggests that coaches gradually increase the athlete's resistance to stress through participation in progressively intense training sessions. The experienced coach can maintain the delicate balance between conditioning and overtraining by carefully monitoring training sessions and insuring that athletes have adequate rest periods following intensive training and competitive efforts.

## Transfer of Training

Transfer of training refers to the fact that skills learned in practice will "carry over" to the performance situation. To this end, coaches should design practice sessions that simulate or duplicate exactly the same conditions the athlete will face in competition. This practice, known as "model training," is essential for maximizing transfer of previously learned motor skills to the performance situation, and is also extremely effective in preparing athletes for the social, emotional, and psychological demands of competition (Vanek and Cratty, 1970).

## Retention

Retention concerns the fact that once skills are learned they will be recalled in future practice sessions and competitive situations. This issue is best addressed by encouraging the overlearning of skills. The following quote illustrates the point: "Repetition is the mother of knowledge."

Athletes must be drilled in the skills they have learned as often as possible to insure that such skills are overlearned and thoroughly ingrained in the athlete's behavioral response system. This drilling insures overlearning and promotes instinctive and reactive (autonomic) responses to cues exhibited in competition. Each athletic skill should have an appropriate set of drills assigned to it which promote maximum retention and recall.

## Mental Practice

Mental practice is a cognitive supplement to training which can effectively enhance the acquisition, transfer, retention, and performance of motor skills. Mental practice is often referred to as "visualization" or "mental imagery" and can be a very effective supplement to physical practice. Although many coaches recognize that a considerable portion of an athlete's performance is "mental," they spend very little time in practice sessions on the mental rehearsal of skills.

Mental training techniques can be introduced into the athlete's practice schedule in a variety of ways, but two of the most common methods are through visualization exercises and video taping.

**Visualization.** Visualization exercises essentially present opportunities for athletes to "picture" themselves performing their skills successfully in practice and performance situations. Films of athletic skills are a form of "structured" visualization which help the athlete conceptualize the appropriate execution of skills. "Free" visualization, by contrast, encourages the athlete to utilize their imagination to rehearse and perform their skills and is usually associated with autogenic training (see Chapter 7).

**Videotaping.** Videotaping can be a very useful supplement to practice procedures by providing athletes with visual feedback regarding their performances. This procedure allows the athlete to visually compare actual performances with how they "think" they performed. Such a comparison will help the athlete to determine what corrections must be made in his or her performance.

## Establishing a Mental/Physical Practice Routine

Coaches often overemphasize the use of auditory feedback in describing skills to their athletes and can enhance their coaching techniques by utilizing videotaping to provide visual feedback. The effectiveness of visual feedback is best characterized by the saying, "one picture equals a thousand words."

A structured mental/physical practice routine which utilizes videotaping to enhance performance would be composed of the following stages:

1. Prior to practice, the athlete views films or videotapes which

demonstrate the correct execution (form/style) of their sport skills. This will give the athlete a "mental picture" of how their skills should be performed. This should be done for 20–30 minutes. To increase the effectiveness of this mental training session include films or videotapes of the viewing athlete performing his or her skill correctly and effectively.

2. Utilizing specified practice drills, the athlete performs their sport skills in the practice session while being videotaped by the coach.

3. The athlete can view his or her performance during or after practice as desired.

4. Upon completion of practice, the coach and athlete analyze the practice session. Athletes can then compare the video tape with the film they viewed prior to practice. Videotapes can be shown in slow motion or shown frame by frame and also compared to sequential photos of the sport skills.

# Coaching Methodology

There are a variety of instructional methods coaches can employ that promote effective skill development. Learning principles inherent in such methods and procedures are concerned primarily with regulation of the practice environment.

The coach regulates practice sessions primarily by determining the optimal amount of practice to conduct and the ideal spacing for these practice periods. The coach can utilize either distributed (spaced) or massed (concentrated) practice sessions to achieve this end.

### Distributed Practice Sessions

Distributed or spaced practice sessions describes a situation where work periods are separated by either rest or some alternate activity. For example, while practicing hitting skills, a baseball player would take five attempts or trials at a time in the batting cage. The player then rests for a period of time, re-enters the batting cage and takes five more attempts. In such a process, each practice effort is followed, and thus, preceded by a rest period during which the athlete may get instruction from the batting coach. Distributed practice sessions are beneficial during the initial stages of skill learning when the emphasis is on the assimilation and execution of correct form, style, or technique.

## Massed Practice Sessions

Massed or concentrated practice sessions provide little or no rest and are utilized in the general conditioning of athletes. This type of practice session is appropriate once a skill has been learned to promote skill retention through repetition (drills). For example, having mastered a particular batting technique, a baseball player will then take a considerable number of swings while in the batting cage (i.e., twenty-five swings before a rest is taken). Repetition of correct motor skill patterns will make them almost automatic. practice will ingrain motor skill patterns.

## Regulation of the Practice Session

The coach should regulate the practice session by controlling the number of trials athletes take rather than the amount of time they spend practicing their skills. Baseball players should take a specified number of attempts (swings) during practice rather than practicing for a specified time frame. This allows for individual variation in the capacity differences of athletes (e.g., experience, fitness levels, skill ability) and helps to counteract the negative effect that fatigue can have upon skill acquisition. If athletes practice in a fatigued state, they tend to make mistakes, practice their mistakes, and form bad habits as a result.

## The Presentation of Skills

Coaches are also concerned with how they present skills to their athletes in the early stages of learning. Skills can be taught either in their entirety (whole method) or broken down into their component parts (part method). In some cases coaches will utilize a combination of these two methods (whole-part-whole method).

**Whole Method of Skill Instruction.** This technique is used to acquaint the athlete with the total movement pattern or at least with combinations of several parts of the movement pattern. The whole method of coaching organizes the learning material so that the learner gets a broad view of all aspects of the sport skill or movement pattern. The whole method of instruction is used in teaching skills which are less complex. It can also help the learner through the initial cognitive stages of skill learning, allowing the athlete to get a "feel" or "picture" how the event is to be performed in its final analysis.

**Pure Part Method.** By contrast, pure part teaching/coaching methods more effectively introduce complex skills and focus attention on only a portion or phase of the entire event or skill. This method is sometimes more effective with less experienced athletes who aren't familiar with certain movement patterns. It allows them to be more focused during the second, fixation learning stage.

**Whole-Part-Whole Method.** Most coaches, however, employ whole-part-whole teaching/coaching techniques, introducing skills in their entirety and then isolating a portion of the overall task. After working on isolated parts, the skills are then practiced or attempted in their entirety. Since most athletes are superior in physical skill learning, coaches should always begin by introducing skills in their entirety, and break them down into their component parts only if necessary.

## Training and Performance Plateaus

Athletes often experience a "leveling off" of their training and competitive performances. This phenomenon can be very frustrating for impatient and inexperienced athletes. Sometimes referred to as "staleness," it can be remedied by utilizing one, several, or all of the following treatments:

1. *Rest*. Remove the athlete from competition and/or the practice setting and suggest an alternate activity or complete rest. Sometimes, the harder you train the more tired you get: the athlete needs to train "smarter, not harder."

   Coaches must recognize that there is a distinct difference between overlearning and overtraining. Drilling learned sport skills is important for retention purposes but over-drilling or overtraining can result in a fatigued and ineffective athlete.

   A break from training and competitive routines will allow exhausted or overtrained athletes to physically and psychologically refuel themselves. The athlete should return from such rest periods refreshed and enthusiastic.

2. *Motivation*. Athletes are sometimes "bored" with aspects of their sport and may feel unchallenged. They can be motivated to overcome such feelings as more interesting learning incentives are presented to them. These incentives can range from extrinsic rewards to the mere increase in attention paid to the athlete by the coach.

3. *Insight*. Athletes may need the coach's advice and expertise to identify "new" techniques or strategies which will help them improve their performance.

## Practice Organization

In order to maximize the effects of training, the coach must organize practice sessions according to a seasonal, weekly, and daily pattern. This cycling of training sessions is referred to as periodization. Periodization is a process of dividing the annual training plan into smaller phases in order to allow a program to be set into more manageable segments and to ensure a correct peaking for the main competition(s) of the year (Bompa, 1985).

A seasonal or yearly training pattern should include a conditioning phase, a skill development and intense stress-adaptation phase, a competitive or "peaking" phase, and a detraining phase.

- *Conditioning Phase* (September to January). This phase would emphasize submaximal forms of training in order to develop a general conditioning foundation for more intensive training.

- *Stress Adaption Phase* (January to April). A period of more intense training characterized by stress adaptation and progressively intensified workloads. This is the phase in which skill learning and development take place.

- *Competition or Peaking Phase* (April to June). This training phase emphasizes quality training tempered by performance evaluations. Rest and recovery are utilized in conjunction with selected competitive tests designed to bring the athlete to their peak performance level.

- *Detraining Phase* (July to August). This recovery phase of training is characterized by "active rest," that is, informal types of conditioning or training. Competitive efforts are de-emphasized during this phase and athletes may even take a complete break from training during this phase by engaging in recreational sports.

Weekly training patterns should provide a blend of the training components such as skill learning and development, conditioning, rest/recovery, and competition. An example of a weekly training schedule is as follows:

Monday      Hard training day emphasizing conditioning

Tuesday     Recovery day emphasizing rest (light workloads) and technique work to learn or improve specific sport skills. Mental practice can also be utilized in this phase.

Wednesday Same as Monday

Thursday    Same as Tuesday

Friday      Rest day prior to competition. Athletes will engage in light workout sessions or mental practice.

Saturday    Competition

Sunday      Complete rest or moderate workout of the athlete's choice.

Daily training patterns should promote maximum learning and retention. They may be organized as follows:

- Mental practice/rehearsal prior to practice

- Warm-up, including review of daily practice goals

- Review, recall and practice of previously learned skills

- Introduction and practice of new skills

- Drill of *learned* skills

- Conditioning

- Recovery and warm-down

- Review practice results, provide verbal and visual feedback, encourage self-evaluation

# General Considerations for Determining Practice Content

Conducting planned and well-managed practices greatly increases the likelihood that individual and team goals will be attained. In preparing a practice plan, Martin and Lumaden (1987, pp. 273–274) suggest the following considerations:

1. Devote some time to conditioning activities;

2. Include drills for skill development appropriate for the skill level of the athletes;

3. Design some skills specifically to accomplish the goals for the season;

4. Set written behavioral objectives for every practice;

5. Identify mastery criteria for practice drills;

6. Vary the practice routines across practices;

7. Ensure that the practice drills and routines program success for the athletes;

8. Plan fun activities as rewards;

9. Try to keep everyone active throughout practice;

10. Ensure that the logistics of who does what, where, and when is planned to include an acceptable coach/athlete ratio and full utilization of the playing facilities.

# Principles of Conducting Effective Practice Sessions

The coach should stress commitment to performance goals, development of skills and athletic ability through conscientious and intelligent practice, and a determination to achieve the potential of each student-

athlete through sport participation. The following principles summarize the concepts and ideas presented in this chapter and can serve as
planning guidelines for conducting effective practices:

1. *Practice does not make perfect.* "Perfect, planned, purposeful practice makes perfect." Coaches are successful by design, not by
   chance. Coaches can utilize sound motor learning and
   performance principles to conduct "quality" practice sessions.
   Athletes can then practice with a purpose and be confident that
   they will play as effectively as they have practiced.

2. *Be aware of the stages the athlete will go through when learning skills.*
   Awareness of the characteristics of the cognitive, fixation, and
   autonomic stages of motor skill acquisition will enhance the
   coach's teaching ability and, ultimately, the athlete's ability to
   learn.

3. *Appeal to all learning modes to facilitate the learning of athletic skills.*
   Provide visual, kinesthetic (feeling), and auditory feedback to
   enhance learning for athletes with varying learning orientations.

4. *Reinforcement, properly utilized, facilitates the learning of athletic
   skills.* Use positive reinforcement in concert with informational,
   instructional, and corrective feedback to insure the best results in
   the learning of athletic skills. Provide athletes with a *"reinforcement sandwich"* to develop the correct motor behaviors (e.g., first
   positively reinforce the athlete, then give feedback—
   instructional, corrective or informational, then use positive reinforcement again).

5. *Individualize practice sessions as much as possible.* The most
   effective learning will take place when the coach and athlete
   work together one to one. We cannot "mass produce" skilled
   athletes since each athlete learns differently. Recognize and
   address individual differences and learning styles among athletes.

6. *For maximum learning and retention, a progressive decrease in the frequency of reinforcement and feedback yields the best results.* In the early stages of skill learning provide frequent and specific reinforcement and feedback. As the skill is mastered reward the athlete only partially or occasionally and provide feedback when needed.

7. *The coach can be the architect of the athlete's performance.* The coach can effect the athlete's performance potential by:

   - targeting behavioral objectives;

   - using positive reinforcement;

   - providing feedback when mistakes occur;

   - rewarding the athlete immediately when skills are performed correctly;

   - linking rewards to correct behaviors;

   - rewarding athletes only occasionally once they have learned a specific sport skill or movement pattern.

8. *Conditioning is an essential prerequisite for successful skill learning.* Coach and athlete must understand the influence of physical stress on skill learning and performance. Although athletes must be ready to perform even when they are physically exhausted, they should avoid attempts to learn skills when they are extremely fatigued. An athlete who attempts to learn and perform skills while exhausted will inevitably make mistakes, practice their mistakes, and therefore create bad habits. Avoid mixing conditioning drills with skill acquisition drills.

9. *Transfer of training, retention, and mental training is an important component of effective practice sessions.* Practice sessions should simulate the exact conditions that the athlete will face in competition (transfer of training) and the coach must continually assess whether practice strategies will "carry over" to

game situations. In addition, overlearning skills by the use of drills will aid the athlete in retaining skills. Mental training, properly integrated into a training program, will enable athletes to retain, transfer, and effectively perform learned skills.

10. *Coaching methodology involves regulating the practice environment for effective learning.* Effective skill learning depends upon the coach's appropriate use of distributed or massed practice sessions. Distributed practice sessions are more efficient for performance and learning than massed practice sessions. Distributed practice sessions provide rest between practice trials which allows the athlete to mentally and physically assimilate novel movement patterns and to integrate them with previously learned skills. Massed practice sessions can also be extremely effective in help- ing athletes with skill retention by having them engage in prolonged drill of learned skills. Massed practice sessions are also beneficial for conditioning athletes.

11. *Introduce skills in their entirety, keep instructions simple, and permit the athlete to try the skill as soon as possible.* Utilize a whole-part- whole teaching approach so the athlete can progress from his or her understanding of how to perform a skill to developing a "feel" for how the skill should be performed in it's final analysis. Although breaking skills down into their component parts can tend to make the athlete too mechanical in their movement pat- terns, it may be the only way for athletes to initially assimilate complex skills and movement patterns.

12. *"Staleness" is a natural occurrence in the skill learning and performance process.* Coaches can help athletes overcome this phenomena by suggesting rest, providing insight, and by increas- ing or varying learning incentives.

13. *Yearly, seasonal, weekly, and daily practice schedules should be planned.* Coaches can "periodize" their training programs to

insure a progressive approach to motor skill acquisition and performance.

## References

Bompa, T.O. (1985). *Practice and methodology of training: The key to athletic performance*. Dubuque, IA: Kendall/Hunt Publishing Co.

Fitts, R.M. (1964). Perceptual-motor skills learning. *Categories of Human Learning*, A.W. Melton (Ed.), New York: Academic Press.

Martin, G L. and Lumsden, J. A. (1987). *Coaching: An effective behavioral approach.* St. Louis, MO.: Times Mirror/Mosby College Publishing.

Oxendine, J. B. (1986). Motor skill learning for effective sport performance. *Applied sport psychology: Personal growth to peak performance*, J. M. Williams (Ed.), Mountain View CA: Mayfield Publishing Co.

Oxendine, J. B. (1984). *Psychology of motor learning*, (2nd Ed.) Englewood Cliffs, New Jersey: Prentice-Hall Inc.

Robb, M D. (1972). *The dynamics of motor-skill acquisition*, New Jersey: Prentice-Hall, Inc.

Selye, H. (1976). *The stress of life*. New York: McGraw-Hill.

Smith, R. (1986). Principles of positive reinforcement and performance feedback. *Applied sport psychology: Personal growth to peak performance*. Jean M. Williams (Ed.) Mountain View, CA: Mayfield Publishing Co.

Vanek, M., and Cratty, B.J. (1970) *The psychology of the superior athlete*, New York: MacMillan.

# The Reality
# of Coaching

# Preventing and Reversing Coaching Burnout

Coaches and athletes have recently become more aware of a stress-related condition which can adversely affect their performance and health, namely, burnout. Burnout results from a build-up of stress over time and this condition is consequently referred to as "rustout."

Work-related or performance-induced burnout usually causes the affected coach or athlete to experience mental, emotional, and physical exhaustion. Such exhaustion can result in negative self-concept; negative attitudes towards work, life, and other people; and a loss of idealism, energy, and purpose. Obviously these attitudes are counterproductive in any profession or endeavor.

The athletic world, with its emphasis upon rewards, recognition, status, and achievement, provides fertile ground for burnout. Individuals affected by burnout "become just too tired to care about anything in their lives." Burnout affects those individuals, both coaches and athletes, who are extremely dedicated, goal-oriented, idealistic, high achievers (over-achievers), highly responsible, perfectionists, and success driven, (Odom & Perrin, 1985).

Coaches are often "all things to all people." Leadership responsibilities encourage them to care for everyone and in the process they neglect themselves. Coaches or leaders are successful because they can set aside personal concerns and seek to meet the needs of their followers. They also tend to overwork and in some cases lose perspective regarding the significance of their sport for themselves, their families, their personal and professional development, and their physical and emotional health.

Although the athlete does not bear the intense responsibilities of leadership, he or she must deal with the pressures of performance expectations, training demands, and continual exposure to the achievement-oriented world of athletics.

This chapter presents an educational overview of burnout and the related phenomena of role conflict. Behavioral and physical symptoms as well as treatment strategies for the coach are presented to aid in the identification, remediation, and reversal of these performance-hindering conditions.

# Recognizing the Symptoms and Causes of Burnout

Physical and behavioral symptoms of burnout have been described by Odom and Perrin (1985, p. 215) as follows:

## Physical

- Fatigue and physical exhaustion

- Headaches and gastrointestinal disturbances

- Weight loss

- Sleeplessness

- Depression

- Shortness of breath

**Behavioral**

- Changeable mood

- Increased irritability

- Loss of caring for people

- Lowered tolerance for frustration

- Suspiciousness of others

- Feelings of helplessness and lack of control

- Greater professional risk taking

Burnout occurs in three stages: the stress arousal stage, the energy conservation stage, and the exhaustion stage. Burnout progresses from Stage 1 through Stage 3, although the process can be interrupted and reversed at any time. Girdano, Everly, & Dusek (1993, p. 57) have developed a self-evaluative check list which describes the symptoms and behavior exhibited in each stage. It is advisable for the coach to review this check list periodically throughout a sport season.

# The Stages of Burnout

### Stage 1: *The Stress Arousal Stage* (includes any two of the following symptoms)

1. Persistent irritability

2. Persistent anxiety

3. Periods of high blood pressure

4. Bruxism (grinding your teeth at night)

5. Insomnia

6. Forgetfulness

7. Heart palpitations

8. Unusual heart rhythms (skipped beats)

9. Inability to concentrate

10. Headaches

## Stage 2: *The Energy Conservation Stage* (includes any two of the following symptoms)

1. Lateness for work

2. Procrastination

3. Needed 3-day weekends

4. Decreased sexual desire

5. Persistent tiredness in the mornings

6. Turning work in late

7. Social withdrawal (from friends and/or family)

8. Cynical attitudes

9. Resentfulness

10. Increased alcohol consumption

11. Increased coffee, tea, or cola consumption

12. An "I don't care attitude"

## Stage 3: *The Exhaustion State* (includes any two of the following symptoms)

1. Chronic sadness or depression

2. Chronic stomach or bowel problems

3. Chronic mental fatigue

4. Chronic physical fatigue

5. Chronic headaches

6. Desire to "drop-out" of society

7. Perhaps the desire to commit suicide

Girdano, Everly & Dusek (1993) emphasize, however, that "burnout is not permanent—it is reversible; furthermore, it is preventable. RELAXATION, PROPER DIET, and PHYSICAL EXERCISE not only help you to recover from burnout, but prevents this problem from ever occurring" (p. 58).

Evidently some individuals' personality characteristics and behavioral patterns may make them more susceptible to burnout. Characteristics and behaviors that may predispose a person to burnout include, perfectionism, being other-oriented, and having a lack of assertive interpersonal skills. Henschen (1986) discusses each of these personality types and their relative susceptibility to burnout:

> Perfectionists are at risk because they are overachievers who tend to set high standards for themselves and others and they may also tend to invest more time and effort on a task than is necessary. Other-oriented people have a strong need to be liked and admired and are often extremely sensitive to criticism. They tend to be generous with everyone but themselves. People who lack assertive interpersonal skills find it difficult to say no or to express negative feelings such as anger without feeling extremely guilty (pp. 328-329).

Burnout-related attitudes were very clearly described in "Where Have All the Coaches Gone?" by Patsy Neal (1977), an outstanding athlete and coach. Representative attitudes of some of the male and female coaches Neal interviewed were as follows:

Too much is expected of a coach. Particularly, I wasn't willing to make the time sacrifice. It seemed my team demanded my life. My life seemed to be totally involved in the game. I wanted more.

I have never worked so hard to gain so little. I am not coaching again because the rewards are not as great as the amount of time invested in the coach's job of recruiting, record keeping, reporting, etc.

I was continually facing numerous pressures for publicity, scheduling, managing, scouting, recruiting, etc. Coaching became almost secondary after a while and I began to coach in an aggressive and tense manner. As you would guess, the reflection by my players was a loss of respect, a great deal of passive aggressiveness and covert hostility. It became a vicious circle—one leading to the other.

These remarks were made by coaches who were obviously in the exhaustion stage of burnout. As a result, of their exhaustion they chose to leave the coaching profession. Essentially, because of its limited rewards and disproportional time demands, the coaching profession is often described as a "labor of love" and coaches must realize that the endeavors which excite you the most, tend to exhaust you the most.

In the final analysis, involvement in athletic activities should be a passion in the lives of coaches and athletes, not the passion. We must strive to prevent passions from becoming obsessions by leading balanced and healthy lifestyles that reflect the ability to work smarter, not harder.

An excellent analysis of the stress-related causes of burnout is contained in a letter written by a university basketball coach who had experienced burnout to a coaching colleague recovering from a heart attack suffered at the end of his competitive season. The letter, written by Jon Kootnekoff, a former Olympian and basketball coach at Simon Fraser University in Canada, provides sound suggestions for the prevention and remediation of burnout which he describes as follows:

RUST OUT (worry, anxiety, and guilt regarding one's behavior, either perceived or actual) leads to BURNOUT or other stress-related conditions (staleness, slumps, role conflict) which if ignored and left untreated can lead to BOW OUT or illnesses such as ulcers and high blood pressure and eventually, death.

Dear Friend:

It has been written that, "a bird doesn't sing because he has an answer, he sings because he has a song." My song may be out of tune, but please allow me to SING!

I must admit that I do not know you completely. To be honest, I do not even know you very well. Even though we first met approximately one dozen years past, we've never communicated with one another on the "gut-level;" like having that oftentimes PEAK communication, when humans are "spilling their guts" or getting into one another's "space. . . . "

Perhaps, like you, I first embarked on my coaching career looking for models to follow, those "guiding lights" whose expertise would make me a "winner." I never attended a coaching school as such. I did, however, register for and attend a multitude of clinics. I traveled far and wide to hear "winners" share their super records, philosophies, techniques, methodology and those big "lifeless X's and O's." To my knowledge, there was never a coach who spoke who had a losing record, because who would come to hear a loser's story?

The main topic of conversation was how to motivate those X's & O's and win–win–and keep winning. . . keeping that record intact. Because, my friend, our society has no place for losers!! And to be classified a winner we had to beat the other guy, by winning over him and making him lose. . .

We exist, oh so very much, on extrinsic motivation. Yes, merely exist and not LIVE: especially if we LOSE, we then merely exist, wanting to redeem ourselves so we're allowed to LIVE once again.

We are motivated to perpetuate our low self-esteem by comparing ourselves and our accomplishments, i.e., our actions, with those of others' as a gauge of our individual worth and importance. Having a conviction that we must prove our worth through superior performance and achievements.

We do not realize that we are invariably doing the best we can possibly do at the time, regardless of our mistakes, unacceptable behavior, or human frailties. We harbor shame, guilt and remorse—and/or self-pity.

We've been conditioned or "brain-washed" to accept or love ourselves and others judgementally, calculatingly, selectively and yes, conditionally!

It is my attitude that we as coaches often neglect or ignore our own needs in order to "serve" others—not recognizing and accepting our own growth and well-being as our number one responsibility. We're obsessed reading someone else's poems and stories of their "REALITIES" and we're expected to fit that mold. For example, a coach is supposed to be all of the following to his players: A father, counselor, minister, psychologist, marriage consultant, and the list goes on! I don't know about you, but I never attended a "how to be a father, minister, etc. school. . ."

Approximately five years ago, I collapsed from fatigue, frustration, anxiety, stress—above all, stress! One of my very close

Polish friends diagnosed my state as going through a premature Polish menopause. Now they call it a "person-pause." Because of that challenging and jolting experience, I was motivated to seek an alternative to my lifestyle and coaching attitude. Please, I'm not stating that it's the only way. I am still searching and changing.

I discovered, much to my inner fulfillment, facts about relaxing and not being uptight, heart rates, physical inactivity and exposure to repeated emotional involvement and how this involvement elevates heart rate and disturbs the autonomic balance necessary for the maintenance of good, total health. It is a truism that the systematic relationships between heart rate and the elements of the game which affect the score, i.e., fouls, performance, errors, turnovers and quick breaks, etc., provide the stimuli for the elevation of the heart rate, and eventually STRESS. . .

Today, stress is the cause of many of our illnesses. It affects our everyday lives and it's not just the cardiovascular system that gets knocked out of line by constant stress. Ulcers are produced by stress when it messes up the digestive system. Also, the skeletal-muscular system gets it—and gives us backaches and tension headaches. The worst part about these is that, when you get them—from muscle tension—the pain makes you tense your muscles even more.

We never, or very seldom, hear these facts discussed at clinics—but mostly those puppet-like X's & O's are presented.

In closing, I wish to empathize rather than sympathize with you. I wish you a good recovery. My attitude/spirit will always feel that you are a "winner." AND, finally, I've written this letter not because I think it's going to do me any good—or to help "shape you up". . . I've written it because I can't help myself!

Without bitterness or malice toward anyone or anything, and without thunderous sincerity and simplicity, I remain

Your Friend Always,

Jon Lee Kootnekoff
Former Head Basketball Coach
Simon Fraser University
Burnaby, British Columbia
Canada

# Strategies for the Prevention and Reversal of Burnout

Once they become aware of the symptoms and stages of burnout, coaches and athletes can prevent and reverse this condition by leading healthy and "balanced" lifestyles. As previously mentioned, such a lifestyle should emphasize relaxation, rest, proper diet, and physical exercise to complement work or training habits.

Coaches and athletes can also prevent and reverse burnout by being realistic about expectations of their involvement in athletics. More specifically, coaches as well as athletes should:

- engage in realistic goal setting;

- focus on success;

- exercise patience in the expectation of results;

- focus on the process approach to athletics (e.g., socialization, skill development) as well as the product approach (winning);

- avoid interpreting results self-referentially;

- and define success realistically after evaluating their talents, abilities, resources, and situations (Odom & Perrin, 1985, pp. 220–21).

Odom and Perrin (1985) have also identified specific educational, recreational, work-related, and social intervention strategies for the remediation and prevention of burnout.

## Educational Strategies

These strategies focus on the creation of an awareness about the need to change behaviors that cause burnout. Education can bring about such awareness and reveal ways in which change can be made. Strategies in this category include:

- time management techniques
- relaxation training
- reading professional journals or newsletters
- and attending clinics and conferences

## Recreational Strategies

The aim of *recreational strategies* is to create restful and rejuvenating diversions for the coach or athlete. Such strategies include:

- daily exercise
- vacations
- alternate interests or hobbies
- taking a "break" or "time-out"

## Work-related strategies

These strategies help the coach meet his or her professional responsibilities in new ways. Such strategies include:

- making on-the-job or field adjustments (e.g., adjust practice and competitive schedules)
- changing jobs, positions, or coaching/playing assignments
- delegating authority and responsibility

## Social strategies

These strategies are meant to generate support systems for the coach. They encourage behavior that can protect or prevent the coach or athlete from experiencing burnout. Such strategies undertake to establish friendly or intimate relationships which allow the coach and athlete to share their personal feelings regarding the demands, stresses, and successes of their profession or performance.

# Role Conflict and Coaching

Burnout can also result from role conflict, that is, the coach's perception of how he or she is expected to behave. Role conflict creates an air of incompatibility between the coach's personal values, beliefs, and attitudes regarding their behavior and the behavioral expectations of external sources such as the athletic director, alumni, athletes, and the media.

Role conflict can have negative psychological, emotional, and physical manifestations demonstrated by the following symptoms or conditions: sense of helplessness, perception of loss of control, insomnia, hypertension, depression, alcohol and drug abuse, anxiety, low job satisfaction, burnout, heart attack, and marital collapse (Perrin, 1985).

The roles most likely to conflict with coaching are those related to teaching and family. In many educational institutions, both on the high school and collegiate levels, coaches are hired as classroom teachers and are expected to handle a full load of courses. Most coaches have family responsibilities as well. Role conflict occurs when they try to meet the expectations associated with all of these roles. For many coaches, the day does not contain enough hours (Coakley, 1986).

When they experience role conflict, coaches react with behaviors which are adaptive and require compromise and sacrifice, or are protective as characterized by avoidance and withdrawal. Individuals may choose to leave the coaching profession because of such conflict. This response can be viewed as a "positive change" or "productive transformation" which may be beneficial in many ways. On the other hand, most coaches will attempt to resolve and reduce role conflict or strain by adopting appropriate cognitive and behavioral strategies which will be introduced later in this chapter (Perrin, 1985).

According to Massengale (1981), the most typical responses to teacher-coach role conflict include:

- ignoring or de-emphasizing the expectations associated with one or both roles
- withdrawing from relationships with other teachers and associating only with other coaches
- increasing loyalty to the profession of coaching and decreasing loyalty to the school and the academic setting
- developing a middle-of-the-road approach by combining the similar aspects of both roles and learning to live with the differences between those aspects that cannot be combined
- dropping out of coaching and concentrating on classroom teaching
- dropping out of both roles and starting a new career

Many coaches also face what might be called coach-family role conflict. Marriage partners may feel that coaching interferes with the husband-wife relationship, and children may feel ignored when one parent is always at school or attending to coaching responsibilities. Although this form of conflict affects both men and women coaches, it is likely that married women with children feel it the most (Coakley, 1986).

Jay Coakley, a prominent sport sociologist, describes the effect coaching may have upon family relationships as follows:

Being a successful coach in a highly competitive interscholastic program requires extreme dedication and time commitments. This, in turn, requires support and understanding from family members. Spouses and children have to realize that their expectations will have to wait until the off-season to be met.

When this support and understanding is missing, coaches are forced to make difficult choices. Either they have to leave one or both roles or take them both less seriously. Such alternatives are seldom satisfying (Coakley, 1986, p.309).

## Resolving Role Conflict

The first step in resolving role conflict, whether it is teacher-coach or family-coach conflict, is to examine one's personal and professional values and goals. Such value and goal clarification can be healthy and is essential for understanding and resolving role conflict.

Once coaches examine and clarify their personal and professional values and goals, they will be ready to engage in cognitive and behavioral strategies specifically designed to prevent and/or resolve role conflict (Coakley, 1986; McGuire, 1984; and Perrin, 1985). Such strategies include:

1. *The coach should garner support for his or her program from those who may have incompatible expectations of him or her.* Coaches should identify advocates among their friends and in the workplace. All leaders are exposed to people who are positive or negative influences. An advocate will serve not only as a valued friend but as an influential person whom the coach can trust and depend upon in any situation.

2. *Coaches should control their programs.* By eliciting some guarantees of autonomy from individuals who supervise their position, coaches can create an impression that they are unapproachable when it comes to taking suggestions about how to do their job. They can demand obedience by telling others to keep their suggestions to themselves.

3. *Coaches should be expedient.* Coaches should exercise expedience in the implementation of policies and decisions and be willing to

compromise in order to reduce the potential conflict which may arise as a consequence of such expedience.

Burnout and the related stress-inducing conditions of staleness, slumps, and role conflict, are very real threats to the physical and emotional well-being of coaches and athletes. Coaches and athletes must realize that these conditions can be prevented by adopting these strategies: EDUCATION—Be aware of the warning signs and causes of each of these conditions and the adaptive strategies one can employ to offset the effects of each condition; REST—Learn to relax; PROPER NUTRITION—Maintain a well-balanced and nutritious diet; and EXERCISE—Be physically fit and active.

# References

Coakley, J. J. (1986). Sport in society: Issues and controversies (3rd ed.), St. Louis, MO: C.V. Mosby.

Girdano, D. A.; Everly, G. S.; Dusek, D. E. (1993). Controlling stress and tension: A holistic approach (4th ed.), Needham Heights, MA: Allyn and Bacon.

Henschen, K. (1986). Athletic staleness and burnout: Diagnosis, prevention, and treatment, In J. M. Williams (Ed.) Applied sport psychology: Personal growth to peak performance, Mountain View, CA: Mayfield Publishing Co.

Massengale, J. (1981). Role conflict and the teacher/coach: Some occupational causes and considerations for the sport sociologist, In S. Greendorfer and A. Yiannakis (Eds.) Sociology of Sport: Diverse Perspectives, West Point, New York: Leisure Press.

McGuire, R. T. (1984). *Effective athletic leadership: Dealing with stress*, an unpublished paper, University of Virginia, Charolettesville, VA .

Neal, P. (1977). Where have all the coaches gone? *Women's Athletics*, 3, No. 4, September/October.

Odom, S. J., and Perrin, T. (1985). Coach and athletic burnout. In L. Bunker, R. Rotella, and A. Reilly (Eds.) *Sport Psychology: Psychological Considerations in Maximizing Sport Performance*, Mouvement Publication.

Perrin, T. (1985). Role conflict and coaching. In L. Bunker, R. Rotella, and A. Reilly (Eds.) *Sport Psychology: Psychological Considerations in Maximizing Sport Performance*, Mouvement Publication.

# The Coach and Family: The Stress of Success

*An open letter from a young coach to the old coach . . .*

Dear Coach,

I've just returned home from our school's annual all sports banquet. As I sat there tonight and watched our athletes proudly receive their usual complement of awards, listened to the many exciting moments of the past year's teams and seasons recounted, and as I saw the love and pride in the faces of dozens of parents and teachers, townspeople and friends, I was once again grateful to be a member of the most special profession on this earth, thankful I was able to be "The Coach."

And as I sat there, my thoughts drifted to memories of athletic banquets and athletes of years past, to my seasons as a player, and to my coaches. But most of all, Coach, my thoughts were of you. I realized how much there was that I'd never taken time to tell you, but that

I so much have wanted to say; thoughts to be shared and questions to be asked. So now, rather than let any more time pass, I'm writing this very long over-due letter.

It's been many years since I first sat in your old office and scrubbed basketballs while you were in the gym at practice. I was in the fourth grade then, my first year as your team manager, and I'll never forget the thrill and excitement of being around the athletes and you, and feeling a part of the team. As did almost every young player, I spent hours and hours looking at all the pictures on your walls, pictures of past teams, champions, stars and record holders, and of course, dreamed of someday taking my place on the wall as a member of future championship squads. I just lived for the day that I could play for you as my coach!

But for me, my dreams went even further. While my friends all had star players in those pictures whom they worshiped and emulated as heroes, I, too, saw a person on those walls who, except for my Dad, was the biggest, most important man in the world to me, who represented everything I wanted to be and do in my life. The man in those pictures was you, Coach, and even as a 10-year-old manager, I KNEW that I wanted to grow up and be for others just what you had been for so many. I knew that I would be a COACH!

Our relationship was always so "special." You gave so much of yourself, of your time and energy and interest. Whenever I needed you, you were there, whether it was with a pat on the back, an encouraging arm around the shoulder, or sometimes even with a good stiff "chewing out". But whatever, I always knew just how much you cared and that you were willing to do everything possible to help me grow into a successful athlete, and, more importantly, into a successful and happy person. I, then and now, considered myself to be the luckiest person alive to have had you be such an important part of my life.

And so, with great hope, enthusiasm and unbounded idealism, I took my first teaching position, and with it, my first steps into the real world of the Coach. My goal was simple—if I could provide for one person what you so abundantly gave to me, then my career would be a success; not my season or my year, but my career.

Now, dozens of teams and seasons later, I have to feel that I have been blessed with the best that any coach could hope to find or have. I have always found the appropriate opportunity or "right door to open" just when I would reach a point in my career where I was ready for, and in need of, a new and greater challenge. And with each step, I relied even more heavily on the ideals and values that I first learned from you.

And my athletes! Oh, Coach, I wish that you could have known them all! They are such a special group, and make it so easy for me to give of myself in the way that I want to be able to give. Together we have shared so many great times that the incredible number of "peaks" make the very few "valleys" seem insignificant, other than to offer us an occasional reminder of reality.

As you well know, the successes and great feelings haven't come easily. I know of no other teams who have worked any harder or more completely to prepare themselves than have ours. Nor, have I ever met a coach who is willing to do more to prepare or promote his team or athletes than I. Oh yes, there have been administrators, teachers and other coaches who believe me to be crazy or a fanatic, and then some who dislike or even resent the enthusiasm and excitement that I feel for what I do. But, never my athletes! They know my commitment to them, their lives and their sport experience. They know that I'll be there to "go to the wall" for them, and in return, they are right there with me! For me, THEY are who count.

Have I found that one athlete who would allow me to measure my career as a success? Obviously, the answer is a resounding YES! Yes, I have found that special "one," but found him in dozens and dozens of different young people who, in fact, gave me far more in return than I ever gave to them. I love it, and I would never trade this for any other profession in the world!

But just as I always used to come to you to talk over any troubles, problems or big decisions that I had, there is another side to my career that is not all that I'd wanted or hoped it would be. Once again, I'm coming to you for counsel and advice.

To put it straight on the line, Coach, the problem rests in my marriage. I guess we just never anticipated all the stresses and strains that the life of a coach would add to a marriage and family. It seems that the more successful my life in athletics becomes, the more difficulties we have at home. We both value our marriage and relationship, but yet things never seem to turn out quite right or as we had hoped. It's just so hard to accept or to figure out, that my efforts in one area bring such success and appreciation, which then is also a major source of conflict in another area. We just never seem to be able to share our lives together.

I have to ask, Coach, did you and your wife and family face the same or similar difficulties? And, if so, how did you best handle them? I always question and wonder, how could I have become so prepared and ready for the other areas and issues involved in being a successful coach, and yet be so totally unprepared for this most vital concern and effect? If I had been better prepared, if we had been more aware of what was in front of us, could we have better been able to combine the career and the family?

Thanks, Coach, for being there once again when I need you. Any thoughts or advice will be greatly valued as I continue to sort through this very trying and difficult issue and time in my life.

But, most of all, I want to thank you for everything you have done for me and for others, and to tell you just how proud I am to be "The Coach," and even prouder that you are "MY COACH"!

With much love and respect,

Many Young Coaches

The stresses and strains of combining a successful career and a successful marriage and family life are certainly not new issues in American society, nor are they unique to the coaching profession. Any reasonably well-read person is very much aware of the rapid, almost epidemic rise in divorce rates in America during the past two decades. Various projections have one in three present-day marriages ending in divorce or separation. Add to this number the countless other couples who become disillusioned with marital or family relationships and who never choose the avenue of divorce, but who also never find the happiness and satisfaction they anticipated when they married. While some of the difficulties can likely be traced to poor choices of marital partners, many are a direct result of the couple's inability to achieve and maintain a workable balance between their personal and professional lives.

As is evidenced in the example of the young coach above, the coach and the coach's family may be particularly susceptible to stress and finding the right balance seems particularly difficult. In fact, the qualities that elicit such great trust, respect, and success for a coach, may also contain the seeds for conflict at home. Idealism, enthusiasm and excitement; desire, determination and dedication; care, concern and compassion; and a genuine love for sport, for the athlete and for the career, are characteristics of most highly successful coaches.

It is this personal commitment, so vital for success in motivating others, that causes difficulty in coaches' own personal relationships away from the athletic arena. After giving so much of themselves to the athletes or the sport, coaches may often have little left for the others in their lives, or at least they may be perceived by their families as having little left for them.

## Advice for the Wife of a Coach

For generations the role of the coach was reserved almost exclusively for men. Wives were expected to be supportive and subservient of coaches' personal and professional needs. The time-honored cliché, "Behind every good man is a good woman," became not only the description of the role of the coach's wife, but the formula for insuring marital harmony. Young women about to marry a coach would regularly be given the following advice:

"Be prepared to be independent."

"Learn to fix late, warmed-up meals."

"Don't nag him about being gone so much."

"Listen a lot."

"Never give him advice on how to coach his team."

"Count on him for as little as possible at home."

"Be patient and understanding."

"Don't ever try to change him or interfere with his career."

"Don't feel sorry for yourself."

"Back him all the way."

"Expect to listen to his complaints after he's had a hard day."

"Don't make him choose between you and sports. You may be disappointed with the choice he'd make."

"Realize that the very nature of his job requires sharing him with the entire community—often to the seeming exclusion of his own family."

While such gems might indeed offer insight into life in a coach's family, and may be useful attitudes or strategies for some women, they clearly are not appropriate for everyone. In this enlightened age, such attitudes and strict role assignments are simply not adequate for personal fulfillment, satisfaction and happiness for many women, whether they are wives of coaches or otherwise. This is not to imply that modern women do not wish to be supportive of their husbands and their husbands' careers; it merely means that they may need more for themselves than the traditional role offered. When such needs are not addressed, difficulties and conflict may soon follow.

## When the Wife Is the Coach...

Of further significance is the emerging role of women in the coaching profession. It goes without saying that there is an increasing number of women serving as coaches. And, as the opportunities proliferate for girls to participate in sports, so will there be an increased number of girls who, like their male counterparts, dream of and plan for the day when they, too, become a coach. The flames of their motivational fires will burn just as hotly and brightly as for the men, and they, too, will be characterized by idealism, enthusiasm, desire, dedication, care and commitment.

By all rights, husbands of coaches should accept similar admonishment regarding the treatment of professional coaches. "Behind every good woman is a good man." However, it is highly improbable that men will enthusiastically accept this rather radical role shift, and yet certainly successful women coaches need and deserve the same support that men traditionally have enjoyed.

We should not overlook the situations where both husband and wife are coaches. With such situations comes the added impact of combining these two careers, or the difficulties faced by single coaches in their efforts to establish close, supportive personal relationships, while combining coaching and dating. Whatever the situation, the question is, "Can individuals, couples and families best cope with the stresses that come with being a successful coach and maintain happy and satisfying personal relationships as well?"

# Paying the Price

Three keys to the success of most great coaches are anticipation, preparation, and dedication to the pursuit of excellence. When preparing themselves or their teams for upcoming seasons or contests, superior coaches are consistently thorough in their anticipation of every possible situation. They then become engrossed in devising and developing appropriate strategies to meet and overcome these anticipated challenges. They dedicate themselves to preparing for success in their athletic pursuits. In sport, this is commonly referred to as "Paying the Price!"

It is only appropriate, then, that the keys to successful coaching—anticipation, preparation, and dedication—might also be employed in establishing and maintaining satisfying, fulfilling, and happy relationships. For young people about to enter the coaching profession, or who are about to marry coaches or prospective coaches, such anticipation and preparation may serve not only to prevent problems and heartaches, but may also set the stage for an even greater level of sharing and love than may otherwise have been achieved. And for those coaches and families who have already experienced such stresses, these keys may help to re-establishing the balance necessary for a full and rich marriage relationship. Hopefully, through this anticipation and preparation, many good and loving people, who give so freely and willingly of themselves in the context of coaching may be spared the personal hurt, disillusionment and despair that sometimes accompanies dedication to this profession.

To be a coach is one of the greatest careers to which one can aspire. Our children need good coaches! Rather, they deserve to have great coaches who are filled with enthusiasm, energy and love, who are dedicated to providing the best possible experience through sport, and committed to not only training happy, successful athletes, but, more importantly, to inspiring and developing proud, motivated, successful, and happy young people. In short, we need coaches who are willing to "Pay the Price" themselves! But, let's try to insure that the "price" is not the destruction of marriages, or the sacrifice of the coach's own personal happiness.

Let us now consider some typical situations or issues which are a part of the coach's world, and begin to anticipate the potential for stress and how it might be best handled for the coach to achieve happiness and success in both their professional and personal life.

# Commitments

Good coaches are generally considered very dedicated individuals; dedicated to their sport; dedicated to their ideals and goals; and dedicated to their athletes. This dedication manifests itself in the coach's strong commitments. The predominate commitments in the coach's life are the commitment of time, energy and emotion.

### Time Commitment

For the vast majority of coaches, coaching is neither their full-time profession nor their primary source of income. They maintain another full-time career (for many it is teaching), and must carry out all the duties and responsibilities that go with that job. Truthfully, few top coaches relegate their coaching position to part-time status. They, in effect, maintain two full-time careers. A routine day for a teacher/coach at the high school level might proceed as follows:

6:00 AM    Awake, dress, eat, leave for school.

7:00 AM    Morning workout for selected athletes; Preparation time for that day's schedule.

8:15 AM    Homeroom

8:30 AM    Classes begin

3:00 PM    Classes end—answer phone messages, attend faculty meeting, tape ankles.

3:30 PM    Practice

6:00 PM    Shower in athletic office and change; leave for meeting of league's coaches, athletic directors and principals; grab a sandwich along the way.

7:00 PM    League meeting

9:45 PM    Meeting over; attempt to avoid small talk and head for home.

10:30 PM   Arrive home; check on day in life of family (if anyone is still awake); look through mail, read the newspaper, watch late news on TV.

11:30 PM   Go to bed; get ready to start another day.

Obviously coaches don't attend meetings every night of the week, although many may average two to three per week. Depending on the sport, other evenings, and weekends may be devoted to scouting future opponents, attending clinics and workshops, or participating in regularly scheduled team contests. Additional time demands are created when athletes seek out the coach after practice for individual help, counseling, or advice.

Even when the coach is able to get home at a reasonable hour, have dinner with the family, and enjoy an evening at home, invariably the telephone will ring. Whether it is a call from another coach, a member of the press, or a parent, it all takes away from the coach's free time.

When one considers that many coaches are involved in two or more sport seasons during the year, it becomes clear that the demands on one's time make maintaining a personal life away from sport very difficult. Vacations, family trips, movies, parties, fixing things around the house, decorating a room, mowing the lawn, or even an evening or two at home together all take time. And, where there is not time to spare, there is not time to share!

## Energy Commitment

As mentioned earlier, successful coaches have a great amount of enthusiasm and energy. To maintain the type of schedule that their jobs demand, coaches must have very deep reservoirs of energy. But realistically, it must be understood that the coach is not super-human, and, just as with everyone else, that energy source needs and demands to be replenished.

It is not uncommon, then, for the coach to spend that rare, relaxed evening at home sleeping on the living room sofa. It may be perceived that the coach has unlimited energy for the team and career, he or she has none left to be shared at home.

## Emotional Commitment

Of the three commitments, this may be the most significant because it is at this level that coaches truly give of themselves. To most effectively function as a teacher, coach and leader, it is essential that a strong bond of trust be established between the coach and the individual athletes. This bond, and the deeply-felt coach-athlete commitments that come from it, transcend the individuals' involvement in sport and touch many areas of the lives of the participants.

Few coaches ever gain the deep commitment and dedication of their athletes without first giving the same of themselves. It is an athletic variation on the age-old question of, "Which came first, the chicken or the egg?" That is, "Do they care so much because they are great coaches, or are they great coaches because they care so much?"

This love and care and concern for the athletes are demonstrated repeatedly by the coach, both in the world of sport and in other areas of the youngsters' lives. Because of the coach's love for coaching, for the sport, and for the athletes, coaches are at risk of making the athletes themselves the focal point of their lives. When not actually working with them, the coach may be talking to others about them, or when alone, he or she may be engrossed just thinking about them.

Coaches love the relationship they share with their athletes, and very often, the more intense the relationship, the more pride and satisfaction the coaches feel. Referring again to the opening letter, the young coach, when speaking of the athletes, says with great assurance and pride, "They know my commitment to them, their lives and their sport experience. They know that I'll be there to 'go to the wall' for them, and in return, they are right there with me. For me, THEY are who count." This is a statement of tremendous commitment and dedication. Athletes and teams deserve nothing less. And yet, when coaches lose perspective, this emotional commitment poses a great threat to the personal happiness of the coach and his or her family.

Marriage and parenthood are also founded on strong emotional commitments, and it is the maintenance and demonstration of these commitments that keeps the relationship strong, satisfying, and secure. When the family begins to perceive that it is not "they who count" but the athletes, the home relationship may begin to disintegrate. Sharing of a loved one's time and energy with others, although often difficult, is much easier and more readily accepted than the sharing of that person's emotions.

Another of the traditional bits of wisdom or advice often offered to young wives of coaches is, "Realize he doesn't love the sport more than you. He just loves both, but in different ways." This may be very appropriate and in most cases probably very true. However, it does place the total burden of responsibility for understanding on the spouse of the coach. The athletes NEVER experience this equivocation from the coach. Certainly, the family members deserve to be free from doubt as to the coach's commitment to them.

# Success—Failure

Every coach faces, from a variety of sources, the pressures of success or failure in one form or another. These pressures may often cause additional stresses and strains at home, especially when they are unexpected or the couple is unprepared for them.

The most common pressure comes from viewing winning as success and losing as failure. This view is expressed in the expectations of the coach, the athletes, the parents, the community, and the administration.

Generally, for most top coaches, external pressures are less significant than the self-imposed pressures. True, for coaches of major sports, failure to win could result in being fired or removed from the coaching position, and the resulting pressures are great. Dealing with this lack of security whether perceived or real, and channeling all efforts to achieve the required level of success, can add to the excitement of the position. It also causes a noticeable drain on the life of the coach.

But, winning is not the only measure of success, and thus not the only source of potential failure. Other common measures of coaches' success are participation, academic achievement, character development and program development.

Where the coach's goals or measures of success and the administration's or community's differ there is additional potential for pressure. The coach may stress the importance of character development, while the "higher-ups" demand a winner. Or, just as easily the coach may desire and emphasize the need to be a winner, in a position where the school or community places little emphasis on winning, or does not approve of the coach's methods.

All of these situations imply the pressures derived from the threat of failure in pursuit of success. It would be naive and irresponsible to fail to mention that success breeds its own form of stress. Although exciting, satisfying and memorable, the State Championship or an undefeated season may give rise to the greatest levels of pressure the coach or coach's family ever experience. The coach who is "lucky" enough to have several consecutive winning seasons may not be so fortunate after all.

# Criticism

No matter how successful they are, at some point, all coaches are subjected to many types of criticism, sometimes warranted, but more often undeserved. The criticism may come from athletes, parents, press, colleagues, fans, administration, or even from friends. It may involve questioning the coach's knowledge, strategy, and coaching skill or, more personal attacks on his or her character and integrity.

Whatever the case, most coaches understand this criticism to be a part of the business, merely one of the hazards of being in the public eye. Although they'd rather never be criticized, their confidence and belief in themselves will again buffer some of the pain of such attacks.

Such confidence does not come so easily for members of the coach's family. For a spouse to have sacrificed so much personally for the coach to be able to serve others, to then have to deal with the lack of appreciation, even scorn, in return for those services can result in very distressing emotional reactions.

# Life Changes

Early in a coach's career, it may be typical for the wife or husband to share almost totally in the athletic enterprise. They attend every game, keep score, act as statistician, take pictures, accompany the coach on scouting trips, plan team parties, and generally share in the entire coaching experience. But for many, this format undergoes a drastic change upon the arrival of children. The wife, now also a mother, finds it more difficult to travel and plan her day or life around the team. In fact, she may no longer even desire to be so involved.

Her husband, the coach, may out of necessity, continue with all of the same activities. Now, however, the coach's sport involvement excludes the spouse. Loneliness and feelings of isolation often result, and the effects of other stresses or conflicts are frequently amplified.

Couples who are unprepared for this transition will almost certainly experience some very difficult and trying emotional times. The seeming unfairness of it all adds to the despair, as two highly valued and honored roles of coach and parent potentially act in opposition to each other.

A new twist on this life change concept involves the difficulties encountered when the wife is the coach. In this case, couples give up some of the times shared together. The wife may have to leave, interrupt, or at least significantly alter her career, and limit the commitments she may have wished to make to coaching.

Men who may find it difficult to believe that a woman might feel such ambivalence choosing between coaching and motherhood, need only respond to the question, "Would you give up your career to become a father?"

## Career Change

Even though making a career change can be exciting, when it involves moving to another community, it is regarded as one of the most stressful events in the life of any family. Coaches are no exception to this.

Attaining that coveted head coaching position at a new school or at a higher level of competition, may very well constitute a promotion, source of pride, and an exciting and necessary step in the achievement of the coach's career goals. But it involves moving from a comfortable home, made secure by many wonderful friends and neighbors, it might be more difficult for the family to share in the coach's excitement. If it also means that the spouse will have to leave behind a rewarding and satisfying career, great care should be taken in making the decision to move and in anticipating ways to fill the void created by the move.

# Dual Career Marriages

For financial and personal reasons, we now live in the age of the dual career marriage. This potentially lucrative and rewarding arrangement may give rise to great personal conflict and distress in the family. Briefly, two possible results of this dual career marriage are:

1. That the coach and spouse, both highly dedicated and motivated to achieve success, 'lose' themselves in their careers, and in so doing, lose their marriage.

2. When one partner's career is a great success and the other's is not, difficulties might arise. These difficulties are increased when the partners' careers are similar because there may be an increased tendency to compare. The desire to prove one's worth or capability may, as a result, become more intense. For example, if both husband and wife are coaches, and one is more successful than the other, there is real potential for personal difficulties. This situation does not need to be considered impossible. But it is, at the very least, touchingly complicated.

# Financial

It is plainly and simply a fact of life in the profession—very few coaches ever get rich, gain financial security, or are even able to live comfortably on their salaries from coaching. Most coaches are aware of this when they enter the field, and might proudly say, "I've never made a decision based on the dollar sign yet, and I don't intend to start now." This, of course, is intended, and generally taken, as a statement of the coach's dedication to a set of values and to an honored profession. In most cases, the statement is also totally genuine.

But there are times in the life of almost every coach, when the frustration and fatigue of committing such great personal resources and receiving so little monetary reward causes him or her to ask, "Is it all worth it?"

Even though the coach may never totally accept the perceived injustices, in most cases the answer would be, "YES"! But for the coach's spouse, who may have less of an intimate understanding of all the satisfaction and personal rewards, but a more direct identification with the family sacrifices that have been made—the 'bare-bones' grocery budgets, the mended clothes, or the unfulfilled dream of the family vacation to the ocean, the same question might be much more difficult to answer in the affirmative. In short, romantic notions about being a coach will do little to ward off the stresses and strains of limited finances and tight budgets.

## The Unplanned Success

Some of our most successful, famous, and respected college or professional coaches never dreamed that they would be where they are in their coaching careers. Some expected to spend their lives teaching math or history and coaching at the local high school. Others saw coaching as a way to stay in sports for a few years before entering the business world. Whether their success is attributed to the coaches' charisma, brilliance, genius, innovative ideas, or the chance to work with talented athletes, chances are good that such high level success was not anticipated when these coaches began their careers.

Certainly, success brings many positive rewards, among them fame, travel, social contacts, and for some, even great financial reward. It can provide an exciting, fast-paced life indeed.

It may also bring an even greater demand on the coach's time, energy, and emotion. The pressure to produce consistent winners, even champions, may become consuming, to the point where sometimes even success is not enough. Frequently, the demands on the coach to achieve a high level of success may become extraordinary. Ultimately the effects of these pressures on the coach may show in the family relationship as well.

While the coach may have consciously and eagerly sought this level of success, being aware of the trade-offs between pressure and personal and professional reward, the coach's spouse and family may not have held similar desires. The public acclaim and interest in their private lives can, and often does, become a great burden to carry.

As each new level of athletic involvement approaches, both coaches and their families must continue to look carefully into the future and attempt to anticipate all of the potential effects, both positive and negative, on their personal as well as professional lives.


## Is a Family Possible?

At this point, one might begin to wonder why anyone would ever consider becoming a coach. It could begin to look as if it were a sure fire route to unhappiness and divorce. While it is not our intention to depict the world of coaching in a negative light, we have attempted to realistically point out or anticipate some of the pitfalls, stressful situations, and sources of conflict which those who enter the coaching profession may confront. This is not to suggest that every coach will encounter each of these situations.

Coaching is a great, wonderful, exciting and rewarding career. To better insure happiness, satisfaction, and success in the profession, coaches and their families must thoughtfully consider and anticipate all aspects of the career. They must endeavor to achieve a balance between their personal and professional lives, where partners support each other. In so doing, they will allow both husband and wife to feel that their lives are productive, fulfilled and shared.

Having dealt with the concept of anticipation, we turn our discussion to the task of preparation. Two major questions for the coaching couple to consider are:

1. How can the husband and wife best avoid or prepare for the stresses of being married to a coach?

2. How can being a coach add to the marriage, making it more exciting, satisfying and a source of happiness?

While some attempt will be made to offer suggestions or examples, the primary purpose of this part of our discussion will be to raise questions for each individual and couple to consider personally. From the outset, one must realize that there is no "cook book" answer, no recipe for success. Each must find their own formula, that combination which works for them, and recognize that even it must retain the flexibility to change as individuals and couples grow together.

## Do You Really Want To Be Married?

Although some may find this discussion inappropriate or unnecessary, for this discussion, the fundamental question which must be answered by every couple is, "Do you want to be married to each other, to spend and share your lives together?" Certainly, if the couple is not already married, it is a much handier and better time to be answering this question. If already married, and especially if children are involved, moral, financial, legal, and religious considerations make this question far more complicated.

A very significant part of the decision-making process is the gaining of a realistic understanding of what life together will involve, of what must be given, and what might be gained. Thus, the need for anticipation. This is, admittedly, often rather difficult as the emotions of love tend to cloud issues, and make all obstacles seem surmountable.

Regardless, it is the positive and affirmative response to this question that provides the cornerstone from which the foundation for a strong, secure, and satisfying relationship may be built. Coaches who have traveled down the road to success and satisfaction in athletics have done so after first deciding, "I want it!" So, too with the family.

Without this profound desire and dedication to be together, to share in and to give to each other's lives, there can be no formula or guideline which will bring satisfaction or success in the coach's marriage relationship. For by definition, satisfaction is merely the fulfill-ment of a need or desire.

## Priorities and Goals

Having decided that they do, in fact, wish to be married, it should be the couple's next task to determine their goals and priorities. This process should involve the personal and professional considerations of each individual, as well as for the relationship and family as a unit.

Much of the future success of the coaches' marriage will be depen-dent on the open and honest communication with his or her spouse. Enough cannot be said in support of the need for good communica-tion between the individuals. If there is difficulty, uncomfortableness, or frustration, the seeking out of sound professional counseling should be encouraged. For many, close friends, another couple, or possibly even an "old coach" may serve in this capacity just as well.

It is essential that each spouse has an understanding of what the other wants from his or her career and from life, as well as what each hopes to give and to receive from the relationship. Utmost care should be given to insure that each is allowed to seek and establish an iden-tity with which they are most comfortable and happy. This may be especially true for the spouse of the coach, who in many cases, falls victim to the "I'm just a nobody" syndrome.

However a coach and spouse choose to combine their lives is fine as long as each feels comfortable and secure. If it works best for the spouse to become totally involved in the coach's career and share in it as much as possible, that's great! If not, then independent interests and involvements must be established and cultivated, while still reserving and maintaining common interests which can be shared. The deter-mination of exactly what will work best for each couple can be deter-mined only by them, as they consider the process of establishing their goals and priorities.

# Time Management

Little more needs to be said regarding the demands on the coach's time. Having established goals and priorities for their lives, the couple must now devise an effective plan for using their time to achieve these desired results. This process may be difficult, and may even force the couple to re-think or re-work some of their previously established priorities.

Although a difficult challenge, time management is a task at which the good coach should be most adept. If you have ever played for or observed great coaches in action, you are aware that their practices are well organized, that everything has a purpose, and that little time is ever wasted. Though they are not always able to accomplish everything that they feel is necessary, they are able to identify those things that are most important and to fit them into the allotted time. Most effective coaches have very well developed time management skills.

This is not to suggest that every minute of every day should be planned. However, coaches do need to plan for time with their spouses and families, as well as time for the teams. And it may also be necessary, to plan for some "free" time.

# Thought Management—Paying Attention

Most top coaches are able to totally concentrate on their game and on practice, often losing themselves in thought about their players or a particular strategy. They often appear as if bombs could go off around them without disturbing their attention.

Many coaches can identify with the following:

1. Getting into the car after practice and driving all the way home carrying on an inner conversation with themselves about an incident that happened in practice, an athlete's problem, or an upcoming game. Then, arriving home and walking into the

house, excitedly discussing the same thoughts with your spouse, only to find that you are soon engaged in an argument.

2. Driving 25 miles to a game or meeting, arriving there and realizing that you can't remember anything having driven there. Total attention has been on the sport.

3. Sitting through a meal either silently or possibly even conversing with others while in your mind your planning entries for an upcoming track meet, scheduling the right opponents for next year's basketball season, or even choosing items for next year's athletic budget.

It is not enough for a coach to manage the time to allow for sharing with the family. Physical bodily presence obviously is not enough in itself. The coach's attention, his or her spirit, must be present and available. All coaches might well be advised to tie a bright yellow ribbon around their steering wheel as a reminder that they're heading home, and a cue to tune out the sport and tune in the family.

Coaches should be aware of the focus of their thoughts and attention, and the effect that wandering thoughts may have on their personal relationships. They might increase this awareness and monitor their attention by regularly asking themselves:

1. Do I replay the last game over and over for days with my spouse?

2. Do I first ask about my spouse's day, or do I first talk about my own?

3. Do I think about my team or practice all the way home in the car?

4. Do I talk about the team or athletes all the time, with everyone, even through dinner?

5. Do I act differently at home after a loss than after a victory?

6. Do I allow losing to cause me to view myself as a failure as a coach and as a person?

Again, it must be reinforced that each coach, each couple with a coaching spouse must find appropriate ways of handling this question of attention.

## Bring the Coach to the Family

While much of what has been written thus far has been directed at both the coach and the coach's spouse, this final section is really intended just for the coach. As always we do not offer a "cook book" approach or a set of "How to ..." answers. Hopefully it will raise some pertinent questions.

It must be recognized that there are many different coaching styles, and even more approaches to a successful marriage. But, whatever your style or approach as a coach, you must ask yourself, "Do I bring the same qualities and strengths to my marriage?". You must also realize, of course, that the marriage and family does not desire or need a coach. They do very much want and deserve "the coach"!

Coaches can never be sure what they will find when they approach a team or a season, especially a new team in a new school or setting. There may be little talent, broken equipment, run down facilities, no money in the budget, a "killer" schedule, or an unbelievable rash of injuries. All coaches face these variables and more at one time or another in their careers, and survive! Many not only survive, but they succeed! They succeed because wherever great coaches go, and no matter what the conditions, they always know that they have the most valuable and reliable key to success with them. They always have - THEMSELVES!! And you had better believe that great coaches know how to get the most from themselves.

How can coaches be sure that they bring themselves to their marriage? Only they can answer that. Some thoughts or questions for coaches to ask themselves are:

# The Coach and Family:
# Ten Key Questions

1. Do we have short, intermediate, and long term goals for our "family team" and am I working hard to achieve them?

2. Do we have a challenging schedule, and am I excited about it?

3. Do I make sure that I find a special time for every member of the "family team" each day?

4. Do I take time after a family "victory" to savor and enjoy the good feelings, or do I push right on to the next contest?

5. Do I sulk over a family "loss" and let it hang on, or do I learn from it and move on to the next win?

6. Do I gain my most enjoyment and satisfactions from the process of marriage, or do I need the marriage "events" for that?

7. Am I as funny and enjoyable at home as with the team?

8. Do I provide strength where and when it is needed?

9. Do I demonstrate my commitments of time, energy and emotion to the "family team"?

10. Do my spouse and family know that they are who counts for me?

## Coach, do you take yourself to your family?

Obviously, those of us who feel great pride in being a part of the coaching profession care a great deal about the development of great young coaches. In this chapter we have offered suggestions and guidance for people entering the field in hopes of helping them to anticipate and prepare for the challenge that the coach and the family must face. This topic is rarely covered or mentioned in coaching preparation programs. It has not been our intent to provide answers, but rather to raise issues and to suggest some approaches to potential problems. If it has caused you to think, great! If it hasn't, you may do well to read the chapter again, or possibly even consider choosing a different profession.

If you are already a coach, or married, or both, you can undoubtedly identify with many of the issues raised here. Hopefully, your consciousness has been raised regarding the ways to increase the satisfaction you feel in your profession, your marriage, and family.

*An open letter in response from the old coach to the young coach . . .*

Dear Coach,

. . . and what pride I feel to be able to start this letter to you like that . . . Dear Coach. . . , for I know how proud you are to be called Coach. But even more, I know how well you wear the title. I've followed your career closely over the years, and no one could be happier or prouder than I.

Your letter meant a great deal to me. Although I doubt that I could have ever been all that you seem to so vividly remember, I will choose to just trust your memory to be better than mine. Thanks!

You're right. We always did have a special relationship, as I'm very sure we always will. And although I wish you didn't have a problem that you needed to share, I'm glad you still know that you can look my way.

You ask, 'Did we have problems with our marriage that you weren't aware of?' My most honest answer is . . . yes, of course we did. I was human . . . just as you are, and now you know the truth about us both! Were our problems the same or similar to yours? I don't know; maybe, but maybe not. It really makes very little difference, as any thoughts or advice I might offer would not be changed.

You've been an emotional, excited and energetic person as long as I've known you, and I confidently hope that you always will be. These qualities have brought you great success in almost everything you've ever attempted. They certainly are serving you well now in your coaching career, as both your dedication and success are hardly surpassable.

But you have not always succeeded at everything immediately. You have always held a firm grasp on reality. Neither sport nor life holds all victories for us, and our set-backs, no matter how difficult, are only temporary.

Have confidence in your own process! Prepare yourself, and then play to be the "winner" in your life that you've always been in sports! Keep the faith! Your life and work have meant so much to so many, and YOU mean so much to me.

Much Love and Respect,
    Your Coach

# Mind at Rest™— A Relaxation Training Script

## "MIND AT REST"

*As you listen to this audio-cassette, you can recognize that you're now learning to relax, deeply and completely.*

You can now simply use your imagination to visualize yourself as you relax. And as you do relax you can begin to observe yourself as though you were watching yourself from a camera mounted in the ceiling, or from a chair across the room . . . You can begin to observe the features of your face. We'll start at the top of your head by relaxing all of the muscles of your body. You can spend a few moments visualizing each

*Printed by permission of Ron Roe, Clinician, Rest™ Seminars, 4200 Meridan, Suite 205, Bellingham, WA 98226*

muscle group and allowing those muscles to respond to your images and affirmations of relaxation. Visualizing now the muscles of your scalp and your forehead, allowing the muscles in your temples, up over the top of your scalp and down the back of your neck, become loose and warm and relaxed.

Observing that your breathing automatically and spontaneously becomes slower and deeper, enabling you to slow down every process of your physical body to a state of deep relaxation. Allow the muscles way down deep in the sockets of your eyes to relax. Be sure that your jaw is able to hang loose and relaxed with your teeth unclenched. As you visualize and see your muscles becoming loose and relaxed, you can experience a corresponding feeling of relaxation and a sensation of warmth as the tissues relax and allow your heart to pump that warm, rich, nourishing liquid to every cell and every fiber and every strand and piece of flesh on your body.

Allowing the muscles across the top of your shoulder, neck the muscles of your chest, down your arms to the tips of your fingers and thumbs. Relaxing and recognizing that as you relax you will always be able to maintain awareness. Any outside sounds become like music in your ears. And if there is an emergency situation external to your reality, you'll be able of course to simply open your eyes and respond to that emergency in a normal fashion. Otherwise the sounds are blending in and assisting you in your relaxation.

Feel the muscles now in the small of your back, in your stomach, the muscles in your hips and lower abdomen, the muscles of your pelvis, all of the muscles of your arms all the way down to the tips of your fingers and thumbs. And it doesn't matter which hand gets warm and heavy and numb first. Avoid trying to control body sensations; simply experience them, observe them, and feel your body as it relaxes naturally and reduces the tension and fatigue and stress that can build up in anybody's physical system. As you exhale, exhaling the residues of fatigue and tension. As you inhale, inhaling pure, fresh oxygen and exhaling fatigue, tension and stress.

Feel the muscles now in your hips, your thighs, your pelvis, down each leg to your knees and into your calves. Relaxing your ankles, tops and bottoms of your feet, all the way down to the tips of your toes. Every muscle, every fiber, every strand and piece of flesh on your body now hanging loose and limp and relaxed.

Repeating simple affirmations to yourself as you relax. "It is now easy for me to relax. It is now easy for me to relax. I enjoy taking the time each day to relax. I enjoy taking the time each day to relax." Feeling the muscles now loose and warm and heavy and relaxed. Your breathing pattern easy, comfortable, and deep. Warmth flowing through every muscle, every strand and piece of flesh on your body. And as your physical body becomes more deeply and completely relaxed, you feel and enjoy discovering that you're able to visualize more clearly, colors as well as shapes. And your ability to maintain these colorful images and shapes in the form of meaningful figures, images, and situations, is improving as you relax more deeply.

With every breath you exhale, you simply give yourself the affirmation, "It is easy for me to relax. I enjoy taking the time each day to relax." Now in order for you to deepen your relaxation, I'd like for you to imagine, visualize a stairway with five steps. Each step is numbered from five to one and in a moment as I count from five to one, allow yourself to enjoy the sensation of stepping down one step per count. And allowing yourself to become twenty percent more deeply relaxed with each step that you descend so that by the time you've reached the bottom of the stairway you'll be twice as comfortable, twice as relaxed as you are this moment.

Five . . . as you step down the step, the stairway leading to a quiet scene which will be your communication center.

Four . . . stepping down another step and allowing yourself to gently drift into deeper levels of relaxation, the images of the stairway clear and distinct in your mind's eye. A pleasing environment that helps you to relax.

Three . . . with each breath and with each step feeling yourself becoming more deeply, more completely relaxed. Finding that your perception is improving and that you're experiencing perception with greater clarity, visually, auditorily.

Two . . . stepping down another step, deeply and completely relaxes.

One . . . close to the bottom of the stairs now, approaching a door that leads to your communication center.

And zero, stepping off the last step, stepping through that doorway into a beautiful, pleasing scene that is unusually appealing to you.
Plants, fresh air. You can see the sky, blue and clear with a few clouds rolling by. And you can hear water running nearby, a stream or river. And as you relax in that scene for a few moments, what you can do is to take some time to communicate to the inner computer images and affirmations that can provide your computer, your inner mind, with an understanding and communication of your desired goals, your desired realities and achievements in life.

So spend a few moments mentally rehearsing and communicating with your inner computer. See yourself enjoying each day, all aspects of your life, more free each day from the self-limiting, distressful reactions that can interfere with and can inhibit anybody's quest for excellence. Mentally rehearse and allow yourself to effectively use these skills daily to prepare at the beginning of each day to put your mind in gear and to set your mind for success. Using these skills during the day for momentary rest and refreshment. And whether it's for five seconds or five minutes, at strategic times during the day, to quiet and clear your mind, to reduce the building tensions and stress and then to be able to relax at the end of your daily activities. To clear your mind and enjoy your own free time.

Communicate these goals, these ideas, these successes to your unconscious mind in your own way using images and affirmations while deeply relaxed.

## Pause here to practice visualization skills for a particular period of time

Now in a few moments to count from one to three and when you reach the count three, open your eyes fully, finding yourself completely returned to the state of waking awareness and able to fully understand and appreciate the effectiveness of using these skills daily, at the beginning, during and at the end of each day. Giving yourself silent, quiet, and deep relaxation time for a few moments once or twice each day to mentally rehearse, to provide your unconscious mind with the images and communication of your needs and goals. And you can effectively use these tools to increase time efficiency, to increase stamina, and to maintain consistency and high quality performance in all aspects of your life.

One . . . feeling yourself now beginning to come up, deeply and completely relaxed, yet feeling refreshed as though you've enjoyed a three-hour sleep.

Two . . . alert, relaxed, revitalized, refreshed, having enjoyed yourself thoroughly. A song in your heart and a smile on your face, having enjoyed exploring your own inner space.

And three . . . fully and completely returned to awakening awareness, rested, refreshed, relaxed.

# Creative
# Concentration Script

## An Actual Creative Concentration Script for Basketball

If we win, we will advance to finals and our season continues. If we lose, our season is over—something everyone on the team does not want to face. On this day we will use the skills we have learned and perform them with unconscious effort. I have been working hard all season perfecting my post-position play. Knowing my role and the task I need to perform will help add to the strength of our team.

It is a long bus ride to the destination for our game. While sitting in my seat I go over mental notes and visualize the things I need to remember in the game. My teammates are relaxed and silent—each preparing for the game in their own way. When we are nearing the gym, we have a team huddle on the bus. This gets us excited and brings a closeness to us.

Getting off the bus, we are soon shown to our locker room. This is where we will change into our uniforms. We hear the opponents in the other room being extremely loud. It is their method of psyching us out. We are able to focus on the task at hand while absorbing the surroundings. After I get taped, I walk out to the court. Each person warms up in their own way. I go through my shooting progression, warming up each muscle in my arm. I can feel the tenseness in my muscles wear down. I also take a few shots inside the key where I'll be shooting in the game. Then I find a spot on the floor and sit down to stretch my legs and back. I feel mentally ready for the contest. My body is stretched and I am conscious of the upcoming event.

Before the warm-up, our team meets back in the changing room. Our coach has written our assignments on the chalkboard—who we will be guarding and their tendencies. Also, our offense and defense and a few last minute reminders. I feel nervous but confident. Our team has a last yell before entering the court. Our lay-ups go in with ease. I am conscious of my every move. The longer I am out there the more confident I feel. The warm-up time has ended and we are back at our bench.

The announcer is calling the names of the starters for each team. My name is called and I run to the middle of the court. I shake my teammates' hands and we all run back to the bench. We have one last team cheer before we walk out to the court. I visualize the jump ball while I'm walking onto the center of the court. I need to tip the ball back towards my left shoulder. I see myself being successful. The opponent and I shake hands. The referee throws the ball into the air and I jump high. I tip the ball on the way up. It goes directly to our point guard. We are in possession. I run down to set up our play. The ball is thrown in to me and I grab it strongly. I take a big step with my left foot to go baseline.

As I drop my foot, I take a power move—power dribble. This gives me room to go up for my shot. My shot goes in with ease. My confidence is high as I run back to defense. A shot is taken and I block out my opponent. I jump high for the rebound. There are many hands fighting for the ball, but I am the one who grabs it. I see it to my chest and make a strong outlet pass. The game is moving along very fast. Each team is trading baskets.

Finally, at the end of the first half, we have pulled ahead by just five. I am tired but my determination is taking over the weakness felt in my body. At half-time we go back to our meeting room. Our coach instructs us of the things we need to do to secure the win. I am told to keep posting strong. I am enjoying the time of rest. My body is calm and ready. My mind is still active, reminding me of the important notes.

We have gained a lead by fifteen in the second half. After about ten minutes our coach subs me out. I am very happy and excited about how our team is performing. When I sit on the bench, our coach hits my hand and says I've played well. I congratulate my other teammates.

There are many substitutions taking place. Everyone gets an opportunity to play. By now the other team has mentally given up. My body is exhausted from the effort I have put in. Sweat is dripping from my face. As the final seconds wear down, we all feel excited and are screaming with excitement. We have won and will advance to the finals. Our season will continue and this will be a great memory in my athletic career.

# Index

# Warde Publishers, Inc.

for additional copies of

# Coaching Mental Excellence

### *It DOES matter whether you win or lose*

*Write:*

Warde Publishers, Inc.
3000 Alpine Road
Portola Valley, CA 94028

*Toll-free order line:*          (800) 699–2733

--------------------------------------------------------

ORDER FORM

Please send me _____ copy(ies) of **Coaching Mental Excellence: It DOES matter whether you win or lose** by Ralph Vernacchia, Rick McGuire, and David Cook at $18.95. (Add $3.00 for first copy and $1.50 for each additional copy for packing and shipping. California residents, add $1.56 sales tax per book ordered.) Make check payable to Warde Publishers, Inc.

Total enclosed = $ _____

Name _____

Organization _____

Address _____

City _____ State _____ Zip _____

May we send information on **Coaching Mental Excellence** to a colleague or associate?

Referral name _____

Organization _____

Address _____

City _____ State _____ Zip _____